Galileo Reappraised

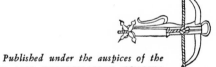

Published under the auspices of the
CENTER FOR MEDIEVAL AND RENAISSANCE STUDIES
University of California, Los Angeles

Contributions of the
UCLA CENTER FOR MEDIEVAL AND RENAISSANCE STUDIES
1. Medieval Secular Literature: Four Essays
2. Galileo Reappraised

UCLA CENTER FOR
MEDIEVAL AND RENAISSANCE STUDIES
CONTRIBUTIONS: II

Galileo Reappraised

Edited by

CARLO L. GOLINO

UNIVERSITY OF CALIFORNIA PRESS

BERKELEY AND LOS ANGELES, 1966

University of California Press
Berkeley and Los Angeles, California
Cambridge University Press
London, England

© 1966 by The Regents of the University of California
Library of Congress Catalog Card Number: 66-15485
Printed in the United States of America

THE CONTRIBUTORS

DANTE DELLA TERZA, Associate Professor of Italian at Harvard University, is a graduate of the University of Pisa and was on the faculty of the University of California, Los Angeles, for several years. Professor Della Terza is now working on two major projects: a book on Tasso, and a critical edition of the De Sanctis letters.

ERNEST A. MOODY, Professor of Philosophy at the University of California, Los Angeles, was previously on the faculty of Columbia University, where he earned his Ph.D. in 1936. His research in late medieval philosophy, logic, and the history of science is represented by a number of well-known books, monographs, and editions of medieval texts.

GIORGIO SPINI, Professor of History at the Magistero, University of Florence, Italy, has, as his particular field of interest, the history of religion. He has been a visiting lecturer in the United States several times. Professor Spini has published extensively on the intellectual-religious history of Italy and also on Colonial American history.

RICHARD S. WESTFALL, Professor of the History of Science at Indiana University, received his Ph.D. in history from Yale University in 1955. He is the author of a book on science and religion in seventeenth-century England and is currently working on a study of Sir Isaac Newton and his papers.

LYNN T. WHITE, JR., Professor of Medieval History at the University of California, Los Angeles, and a graduate of Stanford and Harvard universities, is one of the foremost scholars in the history of technology. In recent years he has been working particularly on the history of medieval and renaissance technology.

PREFACE

On November 6–8, 1965, the University of California, Los Angeles, held a conference commemorating the four-hundredth anniversary of the birth of Galileo Galilei. The papers in this volume were presented and discussed on this occasion. The conference was by invitation only, since its intent was to gather together a group of scholars of Galileo so that they might have a chance to exchange points of view and ideas rather than to present papers to a general public.

The conference was sponsored jointly by the Center for Medieval and Renaissance Studies of the University of California, Los Angeles; the Department of Italian of the same campus; and the *Italian Quarterly*.

In arranging the program of the conference the Steering Committee attempted to present a general view of Galileo's intellectual interests rather than to focus on a single aspect of his activities. Thus, we asked Professor Della Terza to discuss one phase of Galileo's life, perhaps the least known but certainly not the least interesting—that is, his commitment to literature and literary studies. Professor White attempted to reestablish the connection between Galileo's theoretical studies and his equally broad and deep interests in technology. The fundamental problem of Galileo's religious convictions was examined in an original manner by Professor Spini, whose discussion gained particular momentum against Professor Moody's consideration of the intellectual and philosophical context in which Galileo's development occurred. Finally, Professor Westfall examined the particular aspect of force in Galileo's physics, leading us back more specifically to the field of science and of the history of science.

The committee is grateful to all who participated and to the University of California, Los Angeles, for its support. It hopes that this volume will contribute to a deeper understanding of Galileo as both man and scientist.

CARLO L. GOLINO
Chairman of the Steering Committee

CONTENTS

GALILEO, MAN OF LETTERS

Dante Della Terza

SINCE 1896, when an erudite Sicilian, Nunzio Vaccalluzzo, dealt informatively with "Galileo, man of
letters," [1] the subject has been considered in a sense closed
—conscientiously explored and void of mystery. The whole
of Galileo's literary works could in fact be reduced to easily
approachable proportions: [2] there are the two *lecturae
Dantis,* dedicated to the position and importance of the
Inferno; the rough drafts of two comedies, neither of
much merit; several poems in the manner of Francesco
Berni, also of little merit; the *Considerazioni al Tasso,* and
the *Postille all'Ariosto.* The turn-of-the-century literary
critic, committed by the very nature of his own culture to
extensive and impeccable investigation, must have felt himself before a very marginal aspect of Galileo's work in comparison with the main body of his scientific writings. It is
not surprising that after the definitive contribution of
Isidoro del Lungo,[3] a few years after publication of Vaccalluzzo's essay, critical interest shifted. It moved toward
the more fertile terrain of Galileo's scientific pages and the
blending to be found in them between that emotion implicit in any passionately experienced thought and the

[1] Nunzio Vaccalluzzo, *Galileo letterato e poeta* (Catania, 1896.)

[2] See *Le opere di Galileo Galilei,* ed. nazionale (Firenze, 1899), Vol.
IX.

[3] Isidoro del Lungo, "Galileo letterato," in *Nuova Antologia,* Dec. 1,
1899.

clarification needed to defeat all unproven, mythical hypotheses and to affirm new mathematical truths. This shift in the interest of literary critics from one aspect of Galileo's culture, considered incidental and peripheral, to another—a study of the stylistic texture of the major scientific works and its following influence on literature—can be easily observed in a rapid perusal of the titles in every bibliography on the subject. As early as 1911, in the preface to an anthology compiled with Antonio Favaro,[4] del Lungo revealed himself to be a forerunner of this new critical orientation with an exaltation (which seems abstract to later scholars) of the perfect ideal of scientific prose exemplified by the pages of Galileo. Then there is the fundamental contribution of Leonardo Olschki,[5] which tends to emphasize the paradigmatic value of Galileo's linguistic "Tuscan-ness," and, along with Olschki, always on a plane of noteworthy critical rigor, there are the essays of Bosco [6] and Sapegno,[7] the book of Giovine [8]—all three of which are entitled *Galileo scrittore*—and Spongano's very beautiful study of Galileo's prose.[9] Obviously, far from representing an example of intellectual trespassing, which might evoke the righteous wrath of historians of science, these works indicate a need for a concrete analysis and a conception in-extension of the task of literature. This tendency relates directly to that chapter by the major historian of

[4] *La prosa di Galileo per saggi criticamente disposti* (Firenze, 1911).

[5] Leonardo Olschki, *Galileo und seine Zeit* (Halle, 1927). For a discussion of the judgment of Olschki concerning the emblematic significance of Galileo's prose, see Benedetto Croce, *Storia dell'età barocca in Italia* (Bari, 1929), p. 443 n.

[6] Umberto Bosco, "Galileo scrittore," *La Cultura* (1932), pp. 110–118.

[7] Natalino Sapegno, "Galileo scrittore," *Atti e memorie dell'Arcadia*, Vol. I, fasc. 1 (1944).

[8] M. V. Giovine, *Galileo scrittore*, Albrighi-Segati (1943).

[9] Raffaele Spongano, *La prosa di Galileo ed altri saggi* (Messina, 1949).

Italian literature, Francesco de Sanctis, which he dedicated to the "Nuova scienza" in his literary history,[10] where he gave Galileo's personality the weight it deserved.

Still, in recent years [11] there have been doubts whether the last word on Galileo's literary expression has been heard. Did it really represent a moment of relaxation from more urgent and significant scientific preoccupations, or was it related in a more vital way to Galileo's scientific work? When one speaks of a new trend in the interpretation of Galileo's literary works, and of what really counts most in them—the notes on Tasso—one cannot overlook the truly illuminating booklet of the art historian Erwin Panofsky.[12] First, we should note that the relative unpopularity of the *Considerazioni al Tasso* in twentieth-century criticism is bound up with the more mature relaxation of the customary, cumbersome attitude toward the supposed ideal conflict between Tasso and Ariosto, inherited from the academic tradition. The more harsh and obvious Galileo's aversion to the poetry of the *Gerusalemme liberata,* and the more personal his preference for the *Orlando furioso,* the more diffident the attention of the critics to the scientific rationalism [13] or Tuscan provincialism that dictated it. Panofsky's merit lies in having recreated an

[10] Francesco De Sanctis, "La Nuova Scienza," *Storia della letteratura italiana* (Bari, 1925), Vol. II, chap. xix.

[11] Perhaps the first sign of a renewed interest in Galileo's literary work is to be seen in the anthology of his literary writings prepared by Alberto Chiari for the publisher Lemonnier (Firenze, 1943) at the time of the tercentenary of Galileo's death.

[12] Erwin Panofsky, *Galileo as a Critic of the Arts* (The Hague, 1954). Of fundamental importance is the review of this book by Alexandre Koyré which appeared in *Critique,* IX (1955), 835 ff., under the title "Attitude esthétique et pensée scientifique." We find Panofsky's position restated in his essay "Galileo as a Critic of the Arts, Aesthetic Attitude and Scientific Thought," which appeared in *Isis,* XLVII (1956), 3–15.

[13] See for example Ulrich Leo, *Torquato Tasso, Studien zu Vorgeschichte des Secentismo* (Bern, 1951), p. 260.

interest in Galileo's work on Tasso, referring the polemical tone that dominates it to a cultural substratum that is anything but episodic. Panofsky affirms, in fact, that between 1590 (the probable date of the composition of the *Considerazioni al Tasso*) and 1615 Italy and Europe were living through a moment of supreme, if somewhat illusory, identification with the ideals of the High Renaissance, and this trend was manifested in, among other things, the fervor of an incessant polemic against the deformations of Mannerist art. Galileo felt this cultural pressure intensely, so much so that his whole existence, including of course his works, is indelibly permeated with it. Galileo's work on Tasso is full of anti-Mannerist references, as well as a perfect interpenetration between well-chosen, discriminate poetic examples and allusions to the figurative arts, which fully illuminate and explain these examples.

Let us take for example Galileo's reaction to the first stanza of the *Gerusalemme liberata,* which deals with the features of the captain, his successful efforts to liberate Jerusalem, the opposition of the demons, and the errors of his wandering companions. What disturbs the classical tastes of Galileo, trained on Ariosto, is the "representation of broken concepts with no dependence and connection between them." [14] He compares Tasso's poetry to a piece of marquetry—the contours are sharp, the figures dry and hard, lacking the roundness and the modeling of a painting in oil. Here, Panofsky says, Galileo is opposing the pictorial ideal of a Raphael, a Cigoli, or a Domenichino, which he prefers, to that of a Francesco Salviati—an artist much beloved of Tasso—or a Bronzino: Classicism, then, versus Mannerism.

Again Galileo, when he reads the episode in the fourteenth canto of the *Gerusalemme liberata* about the visit of Carlo and Ubaldo to the subterranean world of the

[14] Galileo, *Opere*, p. 63.

magician of Ascalona, is irritated by the tortuous allegory of the voyage, and he formulates a guiding doctrine according to which fable and poetic fiction should either avoid the forcing of symbolism altogether, or else arrive at it with a natural unaffectedness that would be void of "l'ombra d'obligo," [15] the shadow of compulsion. He compares Tasso's allegorical tendency and the distortions engendered by it to those pictures which, when seen from an angle, reveal a human figure, while, when observed from the front, show only chimeras and strange shapes: .... fiumi o sentier tortuosi, ignude spiaggie, nugole o stranissime chimere .... un miscuglio di stinchi di gru, di rostri di cicogne e di altre sregolate figure." [16] In this instance, Panofsky, with his usual penetration, perceives allusions to the pictorial trend that used the distorting perspective of "anamorphosis," of which he gives several examples, such as Holbein's "The Ambassadors," in the National Gallery in London, and most of the work of Giuseppe Arcimboldo.

We can say that what Panofsky proved in his essay, in a manner which seems to be irrefutable, is that Galileo, in his notes on Tasso, championed the cause of simplicity and order, of the separation of the poetic genres, against obscurity, expressing himself in the language of an irresistible cultural force of which he felt himself totally a part. What appears less evident from Panofsky's highly harmonious and circular demonstration is the objective precariousness of the classical character of Galileo's criticism, which is inevitably exposed to a sort of erosion by contiguity through the constant contact and familiarity with the *Gerusalemme*—the major Mannerist text. It is, for example, singular that within a year's time after the publication of Panofsky's essay, an Italian historian, Raffaele Colapietra, in an essay of no small merit, was able to point

[15] *Ibid.*, p. 129.
[16] *Ibid.*, p. 130.

out that in Galileo the critic of Tasso there exists a "taste for the marvelous, for the tragic, which borders on the truculent and Manneristic." [17] The critic had only to shift his attention from Galileo's irreverent polemic to the single-ness of taste which crops up in an attentive reading of the *Considerazioni al Tasso,* for a certain residue of Gi-raldi-Cinzio's poetics of the terrifying and the horrible to show its traces in the very heart of Galileo's discourse.

Should we conclude then that Galileo's work is subjected to two contradictory pressures, one toward poetic splen-dor, the decorative, and the marvelous, and one, much more accentuated and evident, toward realism? Obviously one could object to the formulation of Colapietra's thesis that two and only two possibilities were offered to Galileo: either to refuse the whole Tasso, which would have been difficult, or to accept those verses of the *Liberata* which are close to Ariosto's lucidity in telling a story. Unfortunately, Tasso could write only what is "Tassesco," and Galileo in dealing with Tasso had, in a certain measure, to play Tasso's game. The fact is that, the objective motivation of Tasso's verse being so deceptive, even an innocent description such as the one contained in the line "e l'infinito numero di navi" would convey the amazement of the poet when he is con-fronted with a plurality of objects (here the infinite is viewed as a continuum which patches together, from a subjective point of view, the plurality of the objects), and the intensity of his lyrical emotion, which often has a powerful, crystallizing effect on the narrative flow of the stanza. Should we then incline toward the opinion that Galileo was trapped in Tasso's net and became so involved with him that he could not accept anything from him without compromising the purity of his classical ideals?

[17] Raffaele Colapietra, "Il pensiero estetico galileiano," *Belfagor,* no. 5, Sept., 1956, pp. 557–569.

To give a satisfactory answer to the questions raised, we should take a good look at Galileo's notes on Tasso, and consider them not so much as a striking example of the violent confrontation of two conflicting personalities, or from the opposite point of view, as a subjective and awkward compromise between two ideals of art, but rather as an extreme document of the classical period in the late sixteenth century, as Panofsky theorized.

To the extent that Galileo's text was written in ignorance of the ethical and stylistic torment that led Tasso to the transformation of the *Gerusalemme liberata* into the *Conquistata*, it occupies a position of indifferent equidistance between two crucial moments in Tasso's poetics; inasmuch, however, as it represents a state of mind common to all the followers of the Accademia della Crusca and the intransigent admirers of Ariosto, it also defines itself in relation to the crisis that led Tasso to the revision of his poem. I do not wish by any means to imply that Tasso had before him Galileo's notes, had ever read them or even had any vague knowledge of their existence. I am only concerned with bringing out the weight the classical habit still carried in Tasso's mind, to the point that the theoretical taste of Galileo, the corrector, and of the poet at whom the corrections are directed, end by becoming identical and fusing in the new equilibrium, unstable though it may be, of the *Gerusalemme conquistata*.

The precariousness of the classical background in which Galileo's text fits is shown not only by the acceptance of certain eloquent episodes in the *Liberata*, but by the taste for verbal excess that dominates the polemical pages of the work, by the abusive belittling of the love poetry in the *Gerusalemme*, and by the obscene play on words and double entendre derived from the much-praised Berni and the Florentine comic-realistic "furbesco" style. It is as if

in the expressive pastiche toward which Galileo's criticism
tends, there coexisted, along with the youthful, compan-
ionable imagination and the robustness of his Florentine
style, the predilection for the vociferous elements of a
poetics that expresses the exasperation and hence the ex-
tenuation of its own line of reasoning.

The crisis in Tasso's poetics between the *Liberata* and the
Conquistata is obviously less objective, and is, as is not true
for Galileo, who writes after all in a moment of full, youthful, intellectual expansion, the crisis of an imagination in
its decline. However, in a singular reversal of roles, Tasso,
in the attempt (useless from the point of view of poetic
impact) to put order into the highly contested fabric of his
poem, is obliged to turn to a theoretical zone, the only one
he solidly possesses, which is not far from Galileo's classicism. That his most secret impulses urge him toward solutions even farther removed from the classicism of Ariosto
than that in the first *Gerusalemme* should not prejudice our
interest in the operation he attempts and the poetics that
made it possible.

In an attempt to prove what I have been saying, I will
restate the problem of the relationship between Galileo and
Tasso from the point of view of a concrete analysis of the
texts. Since it would be an error to read the *Liberata* and
the *Conquistata* as a continuous poem born of one mythical
drive, let us propose for the two poems the graphic image
of a broken line, in the center of which we place, as a sort
of objective correlative of Tasso's purging conscience, the
notes of Galileo. Galileo wrote that just as design and color
make good painting, so the choice of words and their expression—"sentenza" and "locuzione"—accompanied by
decorum, make good poetry.[18] It is the ancient admonition
to *ut pictura poësis* that is reechoed a century later, in
truly Galilean terms, in the words Fénelon speaks to the

---

[18] Galileo, *Considerazioni al Tasso,* in *Opere,* p. 76.

French Academy: "On a enfin compris, messieurs, qu'il faut écrire comme les Raphaël, les Garrache et les Poussin ont peint." As for Tasso, he too recalled that the poet is "un pittore parlante," and that what had been denied him by nature in the domain of language and style he could acquire through constant contact with the classics and by a discriminating control of his own vocabulary. *Florentinus nascitur, poëta et orator fit.* Certainly, Tasso says, the vivacity and sharpness of the Florentines is an instinctive gift that is denied others, but is it not perhaps also true that the Tuscans often use carelessly that tongue of which they have haughtily made themselves the guardians? [19] Tasso's criticism of the Accademia della Crusca, entrenched in its defense of Florentine cultural hegemony at a moment when it was living solely in the reflection of past glories, does not exclude an ambitious aspiration on his part for an acquired Tuscanism and hence the temptation to follow the suggestions of the principles of linguistic authority in the revisions of the grammar and poetic syntax of the *Liberata*. As the classical linguistic ideal exercises a constant pressure on his self-destructive sensibility, Tasso is tempted to cut deeply into the stylistic structure of the *Liberata*, with devastating results, although where his model is able from time to time to suggest sensible minor corrections, it can occasionally lead him toward plausible new poetic effects.

To turn to Galileo's text, it has perhaps never been noted that the passages of the *Liberata* Galileo criticizes are all or almost all changed in the *Conquistata*, if they are not suppressed altogether.[20] Now the matter of vocabulary and

---

[19] Torquato Tasso, "Il Gonzaga overo del Piacere onesto," *Dialoghi*, critical edition edited by Ezio Raimondi (Firenze, 1952), Vol. II, v. 2, p. 201.

[20] This is true, for example, of the famous episode of Olindo and Sofronia, much vilified by Galileo, and also of the equally famous pastoral interlude of Erminia among the shepherds (Canto VII, st. 6–18), which seemed to Galileo to be the very negation of epic poetry.

poetic syntax plays no small part in the corrections Tasso makes on the *Liberata,* and it might be interesting to give some examples here, always keeping in mind Galileo's point of view, which we might term that of mediator.

VOCABULARY AND POETIC SYNTAX
("VERBA TRANSPOSITA MUTANT SENSUM")

First, although the principle governing Tasso's corrections in poetic grammar and vocabulary often leads him toward the Tuscan current usage as it was established by the Accademia della Crusca and accepted by Galileo, the corrections in poetic syntax emphasize more the revision and inadequacy of the precept accepted by Tasso in the *Liberata* and refuted by Galileo, namely that "verba transposita non mutant sensum," transposing the words will not change the meaning. I shall give here some examples belonging to both the group of grammatical and that of syntactical corrections.

I

In the first canto of the *Gerusalemme liberata,* stanza 20, the poet, announcing the assembling of the Christian princes gathered together for counsel, expresses himself thus:

> Vennero i duci e gli altri anco seguiro
> E Boemondo sol qui non convenne.

Galileo makes this note: "I do not know if the verb *convenne* may have in our language such a meaning" (p. 65); (all references are to works in the 1899 edition cited in note 2). In the *Gerusalemme conquistata* Tasso corrected it to:

> Vennero i duci e gli altri anco seguiro
> I duci ch'han vermiglie ed auree spoglie.

> (*G.C.* I, 23)

II

Concerning the concluding words of Goffredo's speech:

> Principi, io vi protesto, i miei protesti
> udrà il mondo presente udrà il futuro.
>
> (*G.L.* I, 28)

Galileo exclaims: "Protests can only be made to persons who show themselves to be opposed to what you are trying to do" (p. 66). In the *Conquistata* Tasso substitutes:

> E quel ch'odono in cielo anco i celesti
> Mortali, udite in terra a voi il comparto.
>
> (*G.C.* I, 32)

Here *comparto* ("I share with you") replaces *protesto*, which had disturbed Galileo's practiced Tuscan ear.

III

Again, recalling Goffredo's speech at the point where he tells of the precarious position of the Christian army surrounded by a hostile population, Galileo stops to consider the inexplicable meaning of the following verses:

> Non edifica quei che vuol gl'imperi
> su fondamenti fabricar mondani
> Ove ha pochi di patria e fe' stranieri
> fra gl'infiniti popoli pagani.
>
> (*G.L.* I, 25)

(which we might translate: "Do not build, those who would, empires / on earthly foundations / There where there are few of our land and faith, strangers / among the infinite pagan peoples").

Concerning the third and fourth verses Galileo writes: "I confess ingenuously not to know how to make sense of these two verses, even though I have often pondered on it"

(p. 65). Tasso in the *Conquistata* corrected these lines thus:

> Non edifica quel ch'a gli alti imperi
> Fa mondan fondamento, e quasi in sabbia
> Sperando in suoi cavalli e 'n suoi guerrieri
> Fra' regni d'Asia e l'Africana rabbia.
>
> (G.C. I, 29)

As one can see, the intricate syntax is here completely eliminated.

IV

The poet halts the procession of Christian princes to present the fabulous story of Tancredi:

> È' fama che quel dì che glorioso
> Fe' la rotta de' Persi il popol franco
> Poi che Tancredi al fin vittorioso
> I fuggitivi di seguir fu stanco,
> *Cercò* di refrigerio e di riposo
> A l'arse labbia al travagliato fianco.
>
> (G.L. I, 46)

Galileo does not let the chance go by to note sharply, "It seems he is against grammatical rules and the fact that we should say *cercasse* or *apparisse*, if Cantalicio the grammarian is not to become angry" (pp. 68–69). In the *Conquistata*, for the sake of syntax, according to which a subjunctive would be called for, Tasso eliminates *È fama*, "it is said," thus losing the intense effect of the epic vocabulary of the fabulous, and he begins flatly, "Questi nel dì ch'altero e glorioso" (G.C. I, 58).

V

Now that the Christians have their captain, they long for action. It is not yet dawn and they are already getting prepared to make the last effort to reach Jerusalem:

Già l'aura messaggiera erasi desta
A nunziar che se ne vien l'aurora

. . . .

Quando il campo ch'a l'arme omai s'appresta
In voce *mormorava* alta e sonora
E prevenia le trombe.   (*G.L.* III, 1)

There are here two contradictory movements that Tasso tries to emphasize with his ambivalent sensitivity, never satisfied with clear-cut effects: on the one hand the high and resonant voices of the warriors, anticipating the sound of the trumpets, on the other the impossibility of distinguishing the sense of this collective movement (*mormorava*)—its choral impact. Galileo objects that high resonant voices cannot murmur, that is the province of low, calm voices. It would be better, he suggests, to say "Fremer in voce udiasi alta e sonora" (p. 81). Tasso in the *Conquistata* corrects the lines thus:

Quando ogni schiera ch'al viaggio è presta
Lunge in voce s'udiva alta e sonora.   (*G.C.* IV, 1)

going far beyond the correction of Galileo and eliminating altogether the ambivalent effect in the *Liberata*.

One of the most vivid traits of Galileo's criticism of Tasso is his insistence on the sharpness of the psychological focus, indicative of a taste for rigorously delineated portraiture, free of the capricious quirks of the inexpert hand. A whole category of the *Considerazioni* could be said to be dedicated to this psychological coherence in the design of the characters, which Galileo, and also the Tasso of the *Conquistata*, sought. Let it suffice to mention here two examples of the manner in which Tasso forces himself to react against his customary technique in the name of a more coherent and plausible understanding of human actions.

VI

The Christian camp is by now unified under the leadership of Goffredo. The dukes have approved and the news reaches the warriors. It only remains for Goffredo to show himself to the soldiers in all the prestige of his newly acquired authority:

> Ei si mostra ai soldati: e ben lor pare
> Degno de l'alto grado ove l'han posto
> E riceve i saluti e 'l militare
> Applauso, in volto *placido e composto*
> Poi ch'a le dimostranze umili e care
> D'amor, d'ubidienza ebbe risposto
> Impon che il dì seguente in un gran campo
> Tutto si mostri a lui schierato il campo. (*G.L.* I, 34)

Galileo, after declaring that Tasso fills his pages with useless words, ridicules the demeanor of Goffredo, who shows himself to his soldiers placid and composed, like a little bride who stands before her relatives with pursed lips and lowered eyes (p. 67). What happens in the *Conquistata?* Tasso tries to give greater dignity and coherence to the spectacle, showing us Goffredo in a moment of contemplation during a religious ceremony, from which he returns no longer *placido e composto* but *placido e severo* (*G.C.* I, 38). The field where the warriors will be convoked is transformed from *grande* to *largo,* with a much more theatrical and decorous feeling of anticipation.

VII

On the subject of Argante, who stops to look at the decoration and temper of the sword given him by Goffredo (*G.L.* II, 93), Galileo remarks that this "stare a mirarla così sottilmente" is not at all like Argante, and especially not here, where he should be despising everyone (pp. 80–

81). In the *Conquistata* Tasso eliminates completely this 93d octave of the *Liberata,* and when, further on in the fourth book of the *Conquistata,* the suppressed episode is referred to, he is obliged weakly to correct the verses from the *Liberata:* "Questa sanguigna spada è quella stessa / che 'l signor vostro mi donò pur ieri" (*G.L.* III, 47), to "Questa sanguigna spada è quella stessa / che 'l signor vostro disprezzò pur ieri" (*G.C.* IV, 52).

LA SCATOLA DEL GRANDE
("THE BOX FULL OF BIGNESS")

A final interesting group of examples could be drawn from that tendency of Tasso's toward amplification, which so saddened Galileo. "He begins to put his hand in the box of bigness," Galileo writes, "to season the soup with big chiefs, big bulls, big horses, etc. etc." (p. 79). Reading the two verses: "Ma di vecchiezza indomita e munita / di due gran figli, e pur non fu sicura" (*G.L.* III, 35), Galileo exclaims: "Tocca pur su con quel maledetto grande! Dovevano esser due gran facchini che tanto è in lingua Toscana a dir due gran figli" (p. 88). Now the reduction of this zone of bigness is not foreign to Tasso's stylistic intentions in the *Conquistata,* and there are several convincing examples. For instance, here is how Tasso corrected the verses quoted above: "Ma di forte vecchiezza e ben munita / e pur tra' figli suoi non fu sicura" (*G.C.* IV, 41). And again elsewhere, "tal gran tauro talor ne l'ampio agone" (*G.L.* III, 32), becomes "Così tauro talor ne l'ampio agone" (*G.C.* IV, 38); "E crollando il gran capo alza la faccia" (*G.L.* III, 52) changes to "E crollando la fronte alza la faccia" (*G.C.* IV, 57). The verses: "Quel grande giù, ch'n contra il cielo eresse / l'alta mole d'error forse tal era" (*G.L.* II, 91) becomes "Tal era quel che monte impose a monte / o chi torre drizzò d'error si carca" (*G.C.* III, 89).

However, this tendency to reduce the octave to the narrative line and to simplify the adjectives is in contrast to an opposite, more important and pervasive movement toward amplification, which tips the *Conquistata,* much more than the *Liberata,* definitively toward the baroque. Among the correct judgments Galileo made about Tasso, there is the observation that the poet tended to render subjective the things he described, instead of objectively changing himself in them—"invece di mutare sè nelle cose da rappresentare." The consequence, from the point of view of poetic technique, is the madrigal-like crystallization of the octave—"la discontinovata narrazione"—of the *Liberata,* which reminds Galileo of the ill-famed piece of marquetry, to which he opposes the "narrazione continuata," the narrative fluidity of Ariosto. "Unfortunately for him," Galileo writes, "Tasso limits himself to tossing into the last lines of a stanza a new subject which has nothing to do with what has been said in the rest of it, so that the narrative comes out broken and patched" (p. 123). Tasso uses only one method in the *Conquistata* to react against the crowding of events into the body of a single octave and to reduce the poetic discourse to an organic unity, namely, rhetorical amplification, the baroque dilation and expansion of the narrative flow. One and only one event should dominate the octave, so every other event is pushed out of this metrical space, each one to become a center on its own with its own cortege of epithets and adjectives of no great significance, in a sort of delirious extension of a new expressive system. What Galileo would have said and thought of this end result of Classical poetics, we unfortunately will never know.

Let us turn now to Galileo and the illuminating evaluation of his text on Tasso which Panofsky has given us. It is not the scientist who, with his mathematical rationalism, influences the critic, says Panofsky, but rather the literary man in Galileo who influences the astronomer. Galileo does not, Koyré says, address himself as Kepler does in his *Astronomia nova* to a specialized audience, but writes rather as a philosopher addressing himself to the "honnête homme." [21] Galileo, possessed by an "hantise de la circularité," haunted by the circle, would have had the same invincible aversion to the ellipse theorized by Kepler—with regard to the orbital movements of the planets—that he felt for the distorted perspective of anamorphosis and Tasso's Mannerist poetry. And yet I feel that Galileo, who had refused Tommaso Campanella's invitation to philosophize an absolute system of the structure of the universe in the abstract,[22] would, because of his predilection for concrete research and mathematical truth, have subscribed to the words Descartes addressed to the Marquis of Newcastle in 1648: "Votre imagination qui se mêle importunément dans vos pensées, en diminue la clarté, en voulant la revêtir de ses figures." [23]

What then is the literary impact of Galileo's prose, if the effects of the imagination are excluded with such caution? Is his participation in the literature of his times limited to a classical antipathy for all that is not rational and circular? Or has he perhaps also acquired something from the constant contact with the beloved-hated Tasso, of whom he still speaks late in life, in a letter to Francesco Rinuccini written in 1639? [24] Although my answer would incline toward this second hypothesis, I would like to transpose

[21] Koyré, *op. cit.*

[22] "T. Campanella a Galilei, [Napoli] March 8, 1614," *Opere*, XII, 31.

[23] René Descartes, *Oeuvres*, ed. de la Pléiade (1949), p. 1061.

[24] One should not forget also "Il leggiadro canto del sacro poeta," quoted by Salviati in the fourth day of the *Dialogo de' Massimi sistemi* (Milano, 1953), I, 801. Calling Tasso "sacro poeta," Galileo seems to show a far greater consideration for him than in the youthful *Considerazioni*.

my feelings in an objective, even if marginal, consideration of certain of Galileo's scientific themes, studied in their literary impact. Galileo, in a letter written to Kepler in 1610, ridiculed those men who, maintaining that philosophy is a book like the *Iliad* and the *Odyssey*, search for truth not in nature itself but "in confrontatione textuum," trying with logical arguments to rip the new planets from the sky.[25] Galileo's conclusion in the letter is highly interesting since he uses a well-known literary *topos*, but with realistic intention and aim—"Verum instat nox, tecum esse amplius mihi non licet." Here it is no longer the night of the classical allusion, source of repose, that forces the writer to take leave of his correspondent, but rather the night full of stars which calls the astronomer to his work. We witness here a typical movement of Galileo's mind: the spirit of observation, the love of that which is and can be seen, and his devastating irony for the fables and myths of the sophists. One also recalls that felicitous witticism directed at one of his detractors and plagiarists, Baldassare Capra, who boasted of having been the first to observe the appearance of a new star. "If such a primacy is to be held in high esteem, it would be a good idea for those who aspire to some high degree of glory in the mathematical sciences to pass every night of their life watching vigilantly from the summit of their roofs for the apparition of some new star, so that others more favored by chance may not carry off the honor for such a glorious discovery." [26]

It is this ironic-passionate participation in his own discoveries and the prejudices of his times, so far removed from Descartes' "bene vixit qui bene latuit," [27] that creates what we can call the metaphorical force of Galileo's prose

[25] Galileo, *Carteggio*, in *Opere*, X, 423.

[26] Galileo, "Difesa di Galileo Galilei .... contro alle calunne e imposture di B. Capra milanese," *Opere*, II, 520.

[27] "Lettera di R. Descartes a M. Mersenne dell'aprile 1634," *Carteggio*, XVI, 88.

in his letters and his *Dialogo de' massimi sistemi*. And just as the classicism that, with its absolute purity and self-control, dominates the stylistic texture of Galileo's scientific discourse is, in its gravity, totally alien to the slips into the style of Berni that is typical of Galileo's notes on Tasso, so the occasionally madrigal-like rhythm of his prose, distant souvenir of Tasso's manner, has lost here all its literary cleverness and has become impregnated with the tragic substance of a struggle for life itself and for scientific freedom. When Galileo writes that the intention of the Holy Ghost is to teach "come si vadia al cielo e non come vadia il cielo"; [28] or when he epigrammatically writes sentences of this type: "Che la luna sia per se stessa tenebrosa, è non men chiaro che lo splendor del sole," [29] he communicates to us, through a play on words, the whole meaning of a profound doctrine which impregnates with its truth every verbal relationship, burning out all rhetorical embroidery. It is no exaggeration to say that for this type of language, in which all eloquent relief is sacrificed to the limpid order of the argument, and every argument is permeated with a sharp, bitter wit that is absorbed into the rigor of a meaningful discourse, Galileo came to sacrifice that great instrument for international communication—his clear Latin—more and more through the years. There is no doubt that Galileo tried early in his youth to inject his personal sensitivity into the usually detached and impersonal Latin of the scientific treatise, introducing into it either an animating dialogue,[30] or the highly flavored

[28] Galileo, "Lettera a Madama Cristina di Lorena," *Opere* (Milano, 1936), p. 888.

[29] *Ibid.*, p. 891.

[30] It is interesting to observe that the treatise *De motu*, written in normal scientific prose, changes unexpectedly into dialogue; Alessandro and Domenico, two anonymous strollers, seeking a subject for conversation while they are walking quickly to combat the cold, find it in the subject of the walking itself, in the nature of motion:

"Do. Ego, autem, quamvis, celeri gradu procedam, obsistens tamen rhetorical patterns of the "sublime style." [31] Furthermore, he later attempted to exploit the international range of Latin, using this language in a dynamic prose that reached the greatest skill and scientific precision in 1610 with the *Sidereus nuncius*. This same Latin, which he used for corresponding with Kepler, Tycho Brahe, and Gassendi, seemed to him, however, as early as 1612, to be an inefficient instrument. The letter he wrote to Paolo Gualdo on June 16, 1612, is in fact very moving.[32] While on the one hand he considered it necessary to write in the vulgate so that everyone could read his work, on the other he begged Gualdo and

frigus vincere nequeo, et male in me verificatur tritum illud dictum, Motus est causa caloris. Quapropter, quantum placet, tarde incedamus, atque ad deambulandum extra urbem, de more nostro, proficiscamur quo etiam vel solus proficisci decreveram. Sed qui nostri sermones erunt in hoc mane?

"Al. Quodcumque primum sive mihi in mentem venerit, de quo tamen verba facere iniucundum non sit, de eodem sermonem habeamus.

"Do. De eo itaque quod nuper memoravi.

"Al. At quid?

"Do. Dixeram enim, tritum illud dictum.

"Al. Ah, ah, iam in memoriam redivit.

"Do. De motu itaque sermonem non iniucundum esse arbitror" (Galileo, *De motu, Opere,* I [Firenze, 1890], 367).

[31] An example of this "sublime style" in Latin can be found in the following passage included in the "Frammenti di lezioni e di studi sulla Nuova Stella," of Oct., 1604. *Opere,* II, 278.

"Hic fulgor, tanquam novum e caelo miraculum, tordos atque ad terram demissos populares oculos ad divina erexit. ...

"Testes vos estis, numerosa inventus, qui huc convolastis ut me de hac admiranda apparitione disserentem audiatis; alii perterriti atque vana superstitione perciti, ut intelligant, numquid portentosum prodigium malique ominis sit nunciam; alii mirantes num verum sidus in caelis existat, an vapor ardens prope terram quaerentes; et omnes, de substantia, motu, loco et ratione apparitionis illius, umanimi studio anxie suscitantes.

"Magnifica, mehercle, ingeniorumque vestrorum digna cupido! At, ho, utinam, rei magnitudini ac vestrae expectationi ingenii mei tenuitas possit respondere!"

[32] Galileo, "Lettera a Paolo Gualdo del 16 giugno 1612," *Opere* (Milano, 1953), I, 984.

Sandeli to translate his treatise on sunspots into Latin so that his adversary, Cristoforo Scheiner, the famous *fictus Apelles,* could finally read it.

But who is this *honnête homme* to whom Galileo addresses his scientific discourse in the vernacular? Why does he let his Latin slip away from him? "The reason which moves me," he writes, "is the sight of the young going off indifferently to study to be doctors, philosophers or whatever, many of them being inadept, while others, who would be capable, remain occupied at home or in occupations alien to literature." Here Dante's reasoning in the *Convivio* is revived in a new social and historical context. Like Dante, Galileo felt the necessity of turning to a new class of reader, to the *honnête homme* of his times. Now, precisely in these years when Galileo was turning to a new class of readers and disciples, his own ideas on poetry were being constantly transformed. In the distant times of his activity in the Florentine Academy, in his first lesson "circa la figura, sito e grandezza dell'Inferno di Dante," he had considered it possible to treat a work of fantasy as reality commensurable with the diagrams of the exact sciences. In the period of the *Considerazioni al Tasso* and the *Postille allo Ariosto,* while admitting that the poet roams at will within the boundless fields of the imaginary, he insisted on the necessity, betrayed by Tasso and observed by Ariosto, of submitting poetry to the rules of order, coherence, and verisimilitude. Later, while his mind was more and more absorbed by the task he had set himself, which allowed for no respite, weakness, or contamination of interests, he tended more and more to attribute to poetry a secondary, subservient position. Thus expelled from the world of the real and certain, poetry could even assume the task of celebrating the new scientific discoveries with the metaphorical freedom proper to it. The poets of Galileo then became Andrea Salvadori, Tommaso Stigliani, and Giovambattista

Marino. The latter, in Canto X of the *Adone*, described the results of Galilean research on the nature of the lunar landscape with hyperbolic, exalted metaphors that far surpassed the most turgid manner of Tasso. In a precious display of complicated, verbal skill, the baroque Neapolitan poet showed himself to be joyfully ready to mobilize even the stars to "favellare di Galileo, con lingue di luce ardenti e belle."

But if poetry by now seemed destined to follow the path laid down by Tasso, the scientific lesson of Galileo became ever more rigorous and binding, and its demands on his disciples to observe the separation of the fields of knowledge—to leave to poetry the language of the fable and to seek the essential language of experience—became ever more insistent. But would the nonliterary man, "l'uomo sanza lettere" to whom he addressed himself, be able to follow the line laid down in Galileo's scientific discourse, which was always dominated by a literary elegance void of rhetoric? Galileo's *honnête homme* is no more the "homme meslé," the harmonious, well-bred humanist Montaigne addressed. The *honnête homme* of Galileo's time will in a sense be a disappointing disciple. He will learn either to write scientifically in a style that is correct but lacking in the vibrations of Galileo's perfectly absorbed literary culture, or, in an even more obvious disassociation of interests, he will follow in Marino's footsteps, celebrating the universe Galileo discovered—the lunar landscape and the Medici planets, with all the quibbling, the artifice and acrobatics of the most militant baroque.

GALILEO AND HIS PRECURSORS

Ernest A. Moody

I.

*T*HE NAME of Galileo Galilei is associated in history with events of profound significance to the modern world—with the birth of modern science, with the Copernican revolution, with the dethronement of Aristotle as supreme authority in the schools, and with the struggle against external restrictions on scientific inquiry. Galileo's greatness of character, and his intellectual honesty and devotion to the truth, make him a highly cherished symbol of the human achievements and values he represents. More than any other man of his age, he stands at the crossroads of history.

Until the present century Galileo's originality, as creator of the dynamics that Newton brought to completion, has not been seriously questioned. When Ernst Mach published his *Science of Mechanics* in 1869, he stated without hesitation that "dynamics was founded by Galileo" and, with reference to the kinematic analysis of the accelerated motion of free fall, he said that "no part of the knowledge and ideas on this subject with which we are now so familiar, existed in Galileo's time, but . . . Galileo had to create these ideas and means for us." [1] Soon after Mach wrote

[1] Ernst Mach, *The Science of Mechanics*, trans. by T. J. McCormack (Chicago, 1902), pp. 128, 133.

these words, the *Notebooks* of Leonardo da Vinci were edited and published, and it became evident that the problems of dynamics with which Galileo had occupied himself had been approached in a similar manner by Leonardo, who had used certain concepts, like that of *impeto,* in a way that foreshadowed Galileo's use of them. Similar ideas were then found in the work of Giambattista Benedetti, Nicolò Tartaglia, and Jerome Cardan. These findings suggested the possibility that all these men had some common source of this body of ideas, and Pierre Duhem, the distinguished French historian and philosopher of science, began to search for this source in early printed books on natural philosophy that had come off the presses in Leonardo's time, and which he might have read. Many of these books turned out to be works that had been written by scholastic teachers of natural philosophy at the universities of Paris and Oxford during the fourteenth century—Albert of Saxony, William of Heytesbury, Thomas Bradwardine, John Buridan, Richard Suiseth (the *Calculator*), and Nicole Orêsme, among others. In studying these works Duhem became convinced that the fourteenth-century scholastics of the so-called Nominalist school had conceived and formulated a science of mechanics basically different from that of Aristotle, and strikingly similar in its essential principles to the mechanics of Galileo and his seventeenth-century contemporaries and successors. In a series of volumes published between 1905 and 1916 Duhem presented his findings and developed a radical reinterpretation of intellectual history which has come to be known as "Duhem's thesis." According to Duhem, the analysis of projectile motion and gravitational acceleration embodied in Galileo's *Discourses and Mathematical Demonstrations Concerning Two New Sciences,* involving the principle of inertia and the concept of force as that which changes the velocity and momentum of the body acted on, had been originated by John Buridan in fourteenth-century Paris, and, through the writings of Buridan's pupil Albert of Saxony, conveyed to Galileo, who then gave this dynamic theory a more precise mathematical formulation. Even the latter was said to be derived from another Frenchman, Nicole Orêsme, who had in effect proved that the distances traversed by a body moving with uniformly accelerated velocity increase as the square of the times, by a geometrical form of proof later taken over by Galileo and used to establish the kinematic law of free fall.

Galileo, according to Duhem, was the heir and the defender of this late medieval tradition, at a time when the Renaissance reaction against medieval culture in favor of a return to antiquity had restored the authority of Aristotle in the Italian universities. "When we watch the science of a Galileo triumph over the stubborn Peripateticism of a Cremonini," wrote Duhem, "we, being badly informed of the history of human thought, believe that we are witnessing the victory of a young modern science over medieval philosophy . . . in reality, we are witnessing the triumph, long in preparation, of the science which was born at Paris in the fourteenth century, over the doctrines of Aristotle and Averroes which had been restored to honor by the Italian Renaissance." [2]

A more complete reversal of established views concerning the relation of seventeenth-century science to medieval scholasticism, and to the Italian Renaissance, is hard to imagine. The scientific revolution of the seventeenth century is said to have occurred in the fourteenth century, *within* the medieval schools rather than in opposition to them, and to have been obstructed, rather than inspired, by the Renaissance revival of learning. At stake here are not just a few facts of history, but the whole framework of

[2] Pierre Duhem, *Études sur Léonard de Vinci, 3e Série: Les Précurseurs Parisiens de Galilée* (Paris 1913), pp. v–vi.

interpretation of history. It is not surprising that Duhem's thesis has given rise, during the past thirty years, to vigorous defenses of the traditional view, and to laborious examinations of the evidence on which he based his claims, in an effort to show that his interpretation of this evidence, as well as the conclusions he drew from it, were not warranted. The controversies over Duhem's thesis have tended to be more philosophical than historical, more concerned with the meaning of the facts than with the facts themselves; yet much research into the medieval scientific tradition has been stimulated by Duhem's thesis, and the picture of scientific and intellectual history which we are able to paint today is neither simple nor free from controversy. The medieval precursors of Galileo are here to stay, and cannot be conjured away, though in what sense they merit the title Duhem bestowed on them is a subject of debate. And while most of us continue to believe that the real scientific revolution occurred in the seventeenth century rather than in the fourteenth, the question of what made it a scientific revolution no longer admits of a simple answer.

In this paper I want to examine a rather widely accepted view of the relationship between Galileo's mechanics and that of his medieval predecessors, which may be briefly described as follows: The scholastics of the fourteenth century did, as Duhem claimed, develop a general dynamic theory constituting a science of mechanics different from that of Aristotle. This new dynamics, built around the so-called impetus-theory, became a more or less commonly accepted doctrine in the late medieval period, though a resurgent Aristotelianism reacted against it, in the Renaissance period, especially in the leading Italian universities. It was this fourteenth-century "impetus-dynamics" that Galileo took over and formulated in a systematic manner in his early work, *De motu,* written while he was still at Pisa. But after he went to Padua he became convinced of the inability of this theory to account for the facts, and he therefore made a fresh start on radically different principles, founding the inertial mechanics represented by his *Discourses on Two New Sciences*.[3] This is a plausible account, able to give some satisfaction to all parties. The originality of the late scholastics, in creating a non-Aristotelian dynamics based on a few principles of high generality, is conceded; it is likewise conceded that this medieval mechanics formed a point of departure for Galileo's thought; but the traditional view, that modern classical mechanics was originated by Galileo on *new* foundations that he discovered for himself, is in no degree sacrificed by these concessions to his medieval predecessors. This solution of the historical problem has much to recommend it; it is relatively simple and clear-cut, even ecumenical in spirit. The philosophical perspective it embodies, and which it is intended to support, is one with which I have no quarrel. Its only defect, as far as I can see, is that it is not a true historical account.

II

The core of the problem, from the historical point of view, is what has come to be called, by historians of science, the medieval *impetus*-theory. As generally expounded, this theory supposes that when a stone is thrown upward into the air, the action by which the thrower sets it in motion impresses on the stone a certain power, or ability, by which it continues to move upward after it has left the hand of the thrower; this "impressed power" (*virtus impressa*) grows continually weaker, becoming less and less able to

---

[3] Cf. Alexandre Koyré, *Études Galiléennes* (Paris, 1939), I, 10 and *passim*; A. R. Hall, *The Scientific Revolution* (London, 1956), chaps. 1 and 3; and Anneliese Maier, *Die Vorläufer Galileis im 14. Jahrhundert* (Rome, 1949), pp. 1–6, 132–154.

overcome natural gravity, and thus the ascent is decelerated until gravity finally overcomes the impressed power, at which point the stone begins to fall, increasing its speed as it falls. Aristotle had felt forced to account for such upward motions in terms of propulsion by the air, since he would not admit that a body could move against its nature unless it was propelled by some other body in contact with it. The implausibility of Aristotle's explanation was pointed out by his Alexandrian successors, and both Hipparchus and John Philopon proposed the alternative explanation of propulsion by an impressed power. This theory of projectile motion, taken in itself, is *not* particularly medieval; it was espoused by Greeks, Muslims, and Latin scholastics, as well as by Leonardo da Vinci, Benedetti, and Galileo himself. In this general sense it is not so much a theory, or explanation, of projectile motion, as a rejection of Aristotle's mechanical explanation in terms of propulsion by the physical medium.

In the late thirteenth and early fourteenth centuries a few theologians in Paris discussed the projectile problem and suggested that the original mover of the projectile imparts to it the "impressed virtue" (*virtus impressa*) which remains in it for a short time, then fades away because of being separated from its source. In a manuscript dated 1323 a rather full presentation of this theory, by a theologian named Franciscus de Marchia, is found; it contains various arguments against Aristotle's theory, which were used by later writers down to Galileo himself; but it makes clear that the impressed power that moves the projectile is an essentially temporary quality that is self-dissipating. The word *impetus*, incidentally, was scarcely ever used as a name for this impressed power by any of the Latin writers down to, and including, Franciscus de Marchia. It was introduced as a technical term by John Buridan, a teacher on the Arts Faculty of the University of

Paris from around 1320 to 1358, in connection with an explanation of projectile motion which was significantly different from that of Marchia and the earlier writers.

After rejecting Aristotle's theory by the usual arguments, Buridan said that the projectile, on leaving the hand of the thrower, continues to move in the direction in which it is thrown because the thrower, *by setting it in motion*, imparts to it an impetus that keeps it moving in that direction until the resistance of the air and the opposed force of the body's gravity overcome the impetus. Impetus is described, quantitatively, as proportionate to the velocity and to the quantity of matter (*quantitas materiae*) of the body. But the feature of Buridan's theory which makes it decisively different from that of Marchia is his statement that impetus is a condition of *permanent nature,* such that if no opposed or resisting forces operated to diminish it, it would remain unchanged and keep the body moving indefinitely. Since in the terrestrial regions forces of resistance *are* encountered, and since in heavy and light bodies there *are* natural tendencies to move toward their places of natural rest, the impetus is de facto overcome, and bodies set in motion in this way do not keep going beyond a limited time. This is not because the impetus is consumed by the motion itself, however, but only because it is exhausted by the opposed forces of gravity and air resistance. In the celestial bodies, on the other hand, no such resistances or opposed forces are encountered; so Buridan says, subject to correction by the theologians, that "it could be said that when God created the celestial bodies, He set them in motion in the way that pleased him; and then, from that impetus which he gave them, they are moved to this day, since that impetus is neither corrupted nor diminished, because the celestial bodies encounter no resistance." [4]

---

[4] *Joannis Buridani quaestiones de caelo et mundo,* Lib. II, qu. 12, ed. by E. A. Moody (Cambridge, Mass., 1942), pp. 180–181. The rele-

It seems obvious that Buridan's concept of impetus, as used in his explanation of projectile motion and of the everlasting rotation of the celestial spheres, differs from the earlier concept of a self-consuming impressed virtue in much the same way that the concept of *impeto* which Galileo employed in his mature dynamics differed from the concept of impressed force which he had used in his youthful work *De motu*. It is customary, indeed, to say that when Galileo gave up the assumption of self-weakening of the impressed force and ascribed the retardation of the projectile solely to the resisting forces of the medium and of the gravity of the projectile, that he transformed the "impressed force" theory into the principle of inertia.[5]

Buridan applied his concept of conserved impetus and velocity to the problem of free fall by supposing that the effect of the gravity of the falling body is that of producing increments of impetus and velocity in the body continuously with the time, and since these increments of impetus and acquired velocity are retained and accumulated throughout the time of fall, the movement is one of

vant texts in which Buridan's theory is presented are given in accurate translations by Marshall Clagett, *The Science of Mechanics in the Middle Ages* (Madison, 1959), pp. 505–582, along with a very fine account of the history of the problems of projectile motion and free fall.

[5] Cf. A. R. Hall, *The Scientific Revoluion* (Beacon Press ed., 1956), pp. 86–87. Speaking of the law of inertia, Hall says "it was derived from the consideration of motion in a resisting medium: if the impetus of a body is expended in overcoming the resistance, then in the absence of resistance its impetus and velocity will remain eternally constant." Cf. also Ernst Mach, *The Science of Mechanics: Supplement to the Third English Edition*, trans. by Philip E. B. Jourdain (Chicago, 1915), pp. 25–26: "But it was only when Galileo gave up this supposition of a gradual and spontaneous decrease of the impressed force and reduced this to resisting forces, and investigated the motion of falling experimentally and without taking its causes into consideration, could the laws of the uniformly accelerated motion of falling appear in a purely quantitative form."

continuous acceleration. This analysis, though compatible with that given by Galileo in his *Two New Sciences*, is entirely different from the explanation of free fall he upheld in his early Pisan work *De motu*. In that work, he assumed that the effect of gravity, taken in itself, is a downward motion at *constant* velocity, and that the acceleration observed in falling bodies is owing only to the self-weakening of the residual "impressed force" derived from the agency that raised them, or held them, above the ground. If Galileo's earlier Pisan dynamics reflected a medieval tradition, it was not the *impetus* theory of Buridan that it reflected, but the "impressed virtue" theory of Marchia which was similar to that of Philopon and Hipparchus. And if Buridan's explanation of free fall influenced Galileo at any time, this could only have been during his Paduan period when he gave up his earlier theory and began to analyze free fall in terms of cumulative retention of the increments of impetus given to the body by its gravity.[6]

It was on the basis of the impetus theory of Buridan, and not on the basis of the theory of a self-consuming impressed force such as had been espoused by Marchia, Philopon, and Hipparchus, that Duhem made his claim that the inertial dynamics of Galileo had been originally conceived at Paris in the fourteenth century. Duhem's thesis is not refuted, therefore, by showing that the *virtus impressa* theory of Hipparchus, Philopon, and Marchia, which Galileo adopted in his early *De motu* and later abandoned, was incompatible

---

[6] Cf. my study, "Galileo and Avempace: The Dynamics of the Leaning Tower Experiment," *Journal of the History of Ideas*, XII, 163–193 and 375–422 (April and June, 1951), for an analysis of Galileo's Pisan dynamics and its medieval antecedents. Koyré, *op. cit.*, I, 54–73, expounds this early theory of Galileo in similar manner, but supposes it to represent what he calls the "physique de l'*impetus*, inaugurée, comme toute chose, par les Grecs, mais élaborée surtout au cours du quatorzième siècle par l'école parisienne de Buridan et de Nicole Orêsme" (I, 10).

with the inertial concept of *impeto* at which Galileo arrived in his later analysis of projectile movement and free fall. It would have to be shown that *Buridan's* concept of impetus, and *his* analysis of projectile motion and of free fall, is incompatible with that of Galileo's mature dynamics. I do not think that this can be done, and the strenuous efforts that have been made to show that Buridan's impetus theory did not really differ from the earlier impressed force theory seem to me, one and all, to beg the question.[7]

[7] Cf. Koyré, *op. cit.*, II, 12–13, 19–20, for such arguments. Anneliese Maier, *Die Vorläufer Galileis im 14. Jahrhundert* (Rome, 1949), and *Zwei Grundprobleme der scholastischen Naturphilosophie* (Rome, 1951), has argued the question at length. Leaving aside the psychological and ontological arguments, which are not at issue here, Miss Maier argues that an inertial interpretation of Buridan's impetus is impossible, at least in the instance of the projectile and free fall problems, because even if abstraction is made of resistance by the medium *and* of opposed gravity, there remains an intrinsic *inclinatio ad quietem*, or tendency to come to rest, distinct from the gravity (or levity) of the body. Therefore, despite Buridan's apparent statement that if there were no resistance by the medium or by the opposed force of gravity the projectile would keep moving ad infinitum, Miss Maier contends that Buridan did *not* believe that the impetus would endure forever in the absence of these resisting forces, but that it would be used up by the *inclinatio ad quietem* inherent in every material body irrespective of its substantial form or nature. Now, I have encountered this phrase *inclinatio ad quitem* in Orêsme, who says that the celestial spheres do not resist the intelligences that move them with any inclination to the opposed (rotational) motion or with any *inclinatio ad quietem*. But I have searched all of Buridan's texts relevant to the question, and have never found him using this phrase or positing any such *inclinatio ad quietem* over and above the natural gravity of the body; and I have searched through Miss Maier's books, in which she speaks of this *inclinatio ad quietem* as something assumed by Buridan, and have found no citation or quotation of Buridan's texts, to support what she says, anywhere in these books. What I have found in Buridan's writings, on the other hand, is the repeated assertion that "prime matter" does *not* resist motion, and this would seem to indicate that the *only* internal resistance posited by Buridan is that which is consequent on the substantial form of the body—namely, its *gravitas* or *levitas*.

III

To show that Buridan's analysis of projectile motion and free fall is formally compatible with the analysis of these phenomena given by Galileo in his *Two New Sciences,* and formally incompatible with the analysis given in his early work *De motu,* does not establish Duhem's claim that modern inertial dynamics was created by Buridan and his fourteenth-century contemporaries and successors. What it does show, I believe, is that there was not one common medieval doctrine that can be associated both with Galileo's early dynamics and with the "Parisian dynamics" developed by Buridan. Except for his use of certain arguments against Aristotle's theory that projectiles are moved by the air, which had been used by practically everyone who discussed Aristotle's *Physics* from the fourteenth to the sixteenth century, there is no evidence in Galileo's *De motu* of any awareness of the ideas in mechanics that were first developed in the fourteenth century—no awareness of Bradwardine's exponential reformulation of Aristotle's "law of velocities," no awareness of the kinematic analysis of uniformly accelerated motion developed by Heytesbury and Swineshead at Oxford, no awareness of Orêsme's geometrical formulation of this Mertonian kinematics, and no awareness of the dynamic analysis of projectile motion and free fall proposed by Buridan. Galileo's early Pisan dynamics cannot be characterized as a reflection, and initial tryout, of fourteenth-century mechanics.

There is evidence, on the other hand, in the *Dialogues Concerning the Two Chief World Systems,* and in the *Discourses and Mathematical Demonstrations Concerning Two New Sciences,* of familiarity with ideas originated in the fourteenth century. In these dialogues such ideas are frequently put in the mouth of Sagredo, who seems to have been portrayed by Galileo as representative of the "tradition of the moderns," in contrast to Simplicio, who represents the reactionary Aristotelianism that had become dominant at Padua and other Italian universities since the early part of the sixteenth century. In the *Dialogues,* for example, Salviati asks Sagredo if he is ready to concede that a ball, in falling, continuously gains greater impetus and velocity. Sagredo immediately agrees to this, and then, when asked if the acquired impetus would suffice to lift the body to the original height, he says that it would, if not impeded by an external resistance. Sagredo then gives the example of a ball, dropped into a hole perforating the earth through its center, which acquires enough impetus in falling *to* the center to bring it to the surface at the other side, and he compares this motion to that of a pendulum which, if not impeded by friction, would oscillate forever. These examples, which clearly presuppose Buridan's conception of *impetus* as self-conserving in the absence of resistances, go back to Orêsme and Albert of Saxony, though no doubt Sagredo could have derived them from a later source. At another place in the *Dialogues* there seems to be a very clear reference to a discussion found in Albert of Saxony's questions on the *De caelo,* where Sagredo remarks that the mast of a ship travels further in the same time than the hull of the ship, because it traverses a greater arc. Here Simplicio astonishes his friends by saying, "And thus when a man goes walking, his head travels farther than his feet?," which happens to be a word for word quotation from Albert of Saxony's question 27 on the second book of the *De caelo.* The surprise at Simplicio having made this remark is intended, presumably, to indicate that the Paduan Aristotelians of strict observance, represented by Simplicio, would not have been expected to know the writings of the fourteenth-century scholastics, who were regarded by them as corruptors of Aristotelian doctrine.[8]

The most striking indication of fourteenth-century influence on Galileo's mature mechanics is provided by the Latin treatise *De motu locali* incorporated in Galileo's dialogue on *Two New Sciences*, Third Day, in which the statement and proof of the kinematic law of uniformly accelerated motion is given. At the beginning of this treatise Galileo proudly states that although others had observed that the natural motion of freely falling bodies is continuously accelerated, the extent to which this acceleration occurs had not been determined, and, he adds, "so far as I know, no one has yet pointed out that the distances traversed, during equal intervals of time, by a body falling from rest, stand to one another in the same ratio as the odd numbers beginning with unity." [9] This statement certainly gives the impression that what Galileo takes chief credit for is the determination of the relation between distance traversed and time elapsed in uniformly accelerated motion, and not merely for establishing that free fall is an instance of uniformly accelerated motion. Yet it is only the latter that he can rightly claim, since the relation of distances to times, in uniformly accelerated motion as such, had been determined in the fourteenth century by Heytesbury, Swineshead, Dumbleton, and Orêsme, by means of the so-called Mertonian mean-speed law. Galileo uses this same law as

[8] Cf. Galileo Galilei, *Dialogues Concerning the Two Chief World Systems*, trans. by Stillman Drake (Berkeley and Los Angeles, 1953), pp. 22–23 and 173–174. A note by the translator suggests that Simplicio drew his remark about a man's head moving faster than his feet from the *Enciclopedia Amplissima* of Clement Clementi (Rome, 1624); but its origin is in Albert of Saxony's *Quaestiones de caelo et mundo*, Lib. II, qu. 27 (Paris, 1492).

[9] Galileo Galilei, *Two New Sciences*, trans. by Crew and de Salvio (Dover Publications, New York, 1914), p. 153.

his own basic theorem, and proves it by the geometrical method used by Orêsme. Now this Mertonian theorem, which states that the distance traversed by a body uniformly accelerated from rest is equal to the distance that would be traversed by a body moving for that length of time at a constant velocity equal to one-half the terminal velocity of the accelerated motion, was widely known in the sixteenth century, appearing in at least seventeen printed books current at the time.[10] It is a curious paradox that Galileo's statement and proof of the kinematic law of uniformly accelerated motion, which provided the means for a quantitative formulation of the dynamics of free fall, and which is regarded as the distinctively modern approach to dynamics which makes Galileo's science *toto caelo* different from the qualitative physics of earlier times, should turn out to contain the most definitely identifiable use of fourteenth-century materials in Galileo's work.

Yet it is by recognizing this fourteenth-century influence on Galileo's thinking that problems which have long puzzled students of Galileo's work can be resolved. Why was it, for example, that in 1604 and for five or six years thereafter Galileo felt certain that the distances traversed in uniformly accelerated motion increase as the square of the times, and yet took it as self-evident that the *velocity* increases in direct proportion to the *distance* traversed in such a motion? Why, for that matter, did Descartes also hold to these incompatible beliefs? And why did they think that they could *derive* the $s = \frac{1}{2} at^2$ law from the assumption that velocity is a function of distance traversed? To suppose that Galileo had determined the correct law experimentally, while making the assumption that velocity is proportional to distance because as a geometrician he

[10] Cf. Clagett, *op. cit.*, p. 414, and, for the full history of the medieval background of this kinematic law, pp. 255–418.

thought of motion in spatial rather than temporal terms,[11] is not a convincing explanation; it would take an extremely delicate experiment to establish the law by measurement alone, and resort to a psychological explanation to account for Galileo's association of increase of velocity with increase of distance, rather than time, seems too much like a last resort.

If, however, we suppose that Galileo had been led to reformulate his *dynamic* analysis of free fall in terms of conserved impetus and velocity, by reading Albert of Saxony's writings in which Buridan's analysis was presented, he would at the same time have encountered Albert's *kinematic* interpretation of this analysis according to which the velocity increases in proportion to the distance of fall. In taking over the dynamic analysis Galileo may well have taken this kinematic interpretation for granted as part of the theory. On the other hand, the Mertonian theorem, which correctly describes the relation of distance to time in uniformly accelerated motion, was well known in Galileo's time, although the complicated arithmetical type of proof used by the Mertonian authors was not so well known and certainly not so easy to understand. As many incidental remarks in Galileo's writings indicate, he was quite ready to concede that earlier thinkers had formulated many true conclusions concerning the motions of bodies, but without establishing them by mathematically cogent demonstrations.[12]

In seeking to provide such a demonstration, Galileo had available the geometrical form of proof used by Orêsme, John of Casali, and later authors to show that the latitude of a quality whose intensity is uniformly nonuniform in relation to its extension is measured by its mean degree. Such

[11] This is suggested by Koyré, *op. cit.*, II, 21.
[12] Cf. his remarks in the *Discorsi e dimostrazioni*, ed. nazionale, p. 54.

uniformly nonuniform qualities were represented by a right triangle whose altitude at each point along the base represented the degree of intension of the quality at that point, and whose base represented the "longitude" or "extension" over which these qualitative intensions are distributed. This base or longitude could represent, equally well, a spatial distribution of the quality, such as degrees of heat along the length of a poker cold at one end and hot at the other, *or* the time during which a quality was increased from zero intensity to a maximum intensity by a motion of alteration. The mean-degree law would hold for either instance. Shifting to local motion, the uniformly nonuniform acquisition of a terminal velocity becomes a uniform acceleration, and the same triangular representation was used, with the altitude representing the degree of velocity acquired at each point or successive part of the motion represented by the base or "longitude"; the area of the triangle was then regarded as representing the summation of the velocities corresponding to each point of the base line. It was then easy to show that this total velocity (*velocitas totalis*) would be equaled by a motion at uniform velocity represented by a rectangle whose base is equal to that of the triangular representation, but whose altitude corresponds to that which bisects the base of the triangular figure, and which is therefore one-half of the vertical side of the triangular figure. Taking the "total velocity" as measure of the distance traversed in the whole movement, the Mertonian theorem follows. But it is not immediately evident whether the summation of velocities is a time integral or a space integral. Since this form of proof had been given, in the first instance, as a way of equating nonuniform distribution of qualitative intensities with uniform distributions over the same extension, it was natural to construe the *qualitas totalis*, and derivatively the *velocitas totalis*, as a space integral. This is precisely what Galileo did when he attempted to use this method of proving the Mertonian theorem from the supposedly evident principle that velocity in uniformly accelerated movement increases as a function of distance; a principle that seemed evident to Galileo because the dynamic theory of free fall in terms of successive increments of conserved impetus and velocity had been presented to him in this interpretation by Albert of Saxony. It was I. B. Cohen who proposed this explanation of Galileo's ingenious but fallacious attempt to derive the correct kinematic law from the false assumption that velocity increases with distance of fall, given in his letter to Sarpi in 1604; and the fact that Galileo used the terminology of the medieval theory of intension and remission of qualities, such as "degree," "extension," "total velocity" (*la summa di tutta la velocità*), even after he had corrected his error, is good confirmation of this explanation.[13]

If this explanation is accepted, it becomes quite easy to understand why Galileo believed, in all honesty, that he was the *first* to demonstrate that in the free fall of bodies the distances traversed increase with the square of the times. He had already associated the dynamic analysis given by Albert of Saxony with the Mertonian mean-speed law, but had assumed that his medieval predecessors had sought to prove this law, as he himself for a number of years had tried to prove it, from the assumption that velocity increases as a function of *distance* of fall. But when he finally saw that it could not be proved in this way, and that his predecessors, as he thought, had never realized that the velocity must increase as a function of the *time* of fall, he naturally felt that he was the first to have achieved a cor-

[13] Cf. I. B. Cohen, "Galileo's Rejection of the Possibility of Velocity Changing Uniformly with Respect to Distance," *Isis*, Vol. XXVII, pt. 3, no. 149, pp. 231–235. On Galileo's terminology, cf. Clagett, *op. cit.*, pp. 414–416.

rect demonstration and a true analysis of the way in which gravitational acceleration takes place.

IV

Reverting now to the original question of the historical relationship between the work done in mechanics by the fourteenth-century scholastics and the development of Galileo's mechanics, I would make the following emendations to what I described earlier as a widely accepted view. Although it is correct to say that Galileo's Pisan dynamics reflected *a* medieval tradition—namely that of the self-consuming impressed force as explanatory of projectile motion—it is not correct to say that it reflected the impetus dynamics of Buridan and Albert of Saxony, or for that matter of any of the other distinctively fourteenth-century contributions to mechanics. One early medieval tradition that it *did* reflect, and one of lasting importance in the development of Galileo's own mechanics, was that of the Muslim philosopher Ibn-Badja, known as Avempace, whose view that resistance by a medium is not an essential factor or condition of the motion of terrestrial bodies was adopted by Galileo at Pisa, and never abandoned. It was this that enabled Galileo to generalize Buridan's impetus theory and transform it into a general inertial dynamics.[14]

Second, it seems evident to me that during his Paduan period Galileo *was* influenced by ideas that had been developed in the fourteenth century at Paris and at Oxford—by Buridan's analysis of projectile motion and free fall in terms of conserved impetus and velocity, by the Mertonian kinematic analysis of accelerated motion, by the method of graphic representation of qualitative intensions and extensions used by Orêsme and Casali, and very likely by the

[14] Cf. my study, "Galileo and Avempace," *Journal of the History of Ideas*, Vol. XII, nos. 2–3, pp. 163–193, 375–422.

fourteenth-century treatments of infinity and continuity which were closely associated with these other contributions. In what form, or through what books, these ideas were conveyed to Galileo, are questions that, if answerable in whole or in part, would cast a good deal of light on the way Galileo's thinking developed. If historians of science had given more time to historical research on this problem, instead of engaging in a priori debates over the validity or invalidity of Duhem's thesis, better insight into the nature of Galileo's scientific achievements might well have been gained.

These conclusions may seem to support Duhem's thesis. To the extent that Duhem claimed that the ideas of the fourteenth-century Parisians and Mertonians played an important part in the development of Galileo's mechanics, his thesis is supported. But the further claim that the modern science of mechanics was "founded" two hundred years before Galileo's birth, is certainly mistaken. Not because the fourteenth-century scholastics did not provide ideas and some of the mathematical means Galileo was able to use, and in fact did use, in building his new science, but because in the fourteenth century these ideas and means were *not* so used. In their fourteenth-century occurrence these ideas were scattered superstructures erected on the edifice of Aristotelian physics and cosmology, each part added by a different person or group in isolation from the other parts, so that they were never put together, and never made into a foundation for a new science, by *any* medieval scholastic. Bradwardine and his Mertonian disciples, though quite original in grasping the notion of instantaneous velocity and in achieving an abstract mathematical analysis of uniformly accelerated motion, had no sympathy at all for the dynamic analysis of projectile motion and free fall that was developed by Buridan; their dynamics was that of Aristotle and Averroes. Buridan, whose impetus concept, as used in analyzing projectile motion and free fall, had the real potentiality of being generalized and made the foundation of a new dynamics, did *not* generalize it. He made no effort to eliminate the incoherence between his impetus theory and the Aristotelian doctrine that resistance by the medium is essential to the occurrence of motion by terrestrial bodies. This Aristotelian doctrine he accepted, and along with it the Aristotelian "law of velocities" as it had been reformulated by Bradwardine.[15] Why these fourteenth-century scholastics did not exploit the new ideas they had worked out for special cases, and build a new science that would replace the Aristotelian physics and cosmology, may well be asked. I would suggest that, as teachers in universities whose philosophical curriculum was built out of the books of Aristotle, they had neither opportunity nor motivation to overhaul; their job was to make the best sense they could out of their textbooks, not to abolish them.

From these considerations I draw my third conclusion that, contrary to widely accepted opinion, there was no such thing as a fourteenth-century science of mechanics in the sense of a general theory of local motion applicable throughout nature, and based on a few unified principles. By searching the literature of late medieval physics for just those ideas and those pieces of quantitative analysis that turned out, three centuries later, to be important in seventeenth-century mechanics, one can find them; and one can construct, as Duhem did, a "medieval science of mechanics" that *appears* to form a coherent whole and to

[15] Cf. Clagett, *op cit.*, pp. 421–503, concerning Bradwardine's peripatetic dynamics and his reformulation of Aristotle's law of velocities. Duhem *op cit.*, pp. 432–439, describes the rejection, by the Oxford scholastics, of the impetus dynamics. Buridan's acceptance of the Aristotelian thesis that resistance by a medium is essential to motion at finite velocity, by terrestrial bodies, is evident in his *Quaestiones in libros physicorum* (Paris, 1509), fols. lxxiii *recto*, lxxvi *verso*.

be built on new foundations replacing those of Aristotle's physics. But this is an illusion, and an anachronistic fiction, which we are able to construct only because Galileo and Newton gave us the pattern by which to select the right pieces and put them together. It is a fiction, not because these isolated theories and pieces of analysis conceived in the fourteenth century as a means of resolving difficulties in Aristotle's physics were not *capable* of being made into foundations of a new mechanics. It is a fiction simply because in the fourteenth century these ideas were *not* made into fundamental principles of a new science, were *not* brought together into a coherent unity, and were *not* generalized to bring about abandonment of incompatible doctrines accepted from Aristotle. It was Galileo who did these things, and it was this doing that merits him the title he has held for three centuries, that of founder of modern mechanics. He did not create his mechanics (nor that of Newton as some seem to suppose) out of thin air, and to this extent Duhem is certainly right. But he conceived the *kind* of science that became classical mechanics, using the materials available to him and building his new science with the foundations in the right place. This his medieval predecessors did not do, and did not even try to do. In this achievement Galileo had no precursors among his medieval predecessors.

THE RATIONALE OF GALILEO'S RELIGIOUSNESS

Giorgio Spini

$\mathcal{G}$ALILEO'S approach to religion is still a highly controversial topic among scholars. In recent years Galileo has been labeled as a Catholic by some, as a forerunner of modern secularism by others; or, in the words of the late Professor Banfi, as lacking any interest at all in properly religious problems. I am not sure that the problem has been brought nearer its solution by the use of such vague words as "Catholic" or "secularist." Both Pascal and the Jesuits were Catholic, however much they cordially detested each other; in our times, both General Franco and the late President Kennedy were Catholic; however, few Americans would admit that these men had much in common. Inversely, Cremonini's philosophy was as "secularistic" as it was the opposite to Galileo's. But I am far from presuming to say the last word in this controversy. When the most competent scholars draw the most contradictory conclusions from the same available evidence, it is a sign that the data are insufficient or insufficiently clear. We must be honest enough and humble enough to confess that our sources of information about Galileo's religiousness do not always allow us to reach a certainty beyond all reasonable doubt.

After all, Galileo is no exception to this point of view. One has but to remember the centuries-old discussions of

the historians on the real meaning of Campanella's philosophy, or on Sarpi's stand between Catholicism and Protestantism. The last thing on which seventeenth-century Italians dared to freely express their minds was religious
matters. I am afraid that the best methodological introduction to seventeenth-century Italian religious history is
still a story that circulated in Italy under fascism. There
was an unhappy man who wanted to put an end to his life.
However, he preferred to have himself killed by somebody
else than to take the trouble of committing suicide. Therefore, one day when he saw a column of fascist militia pa-
rading in a street, he began to shout insults against fascism
and the Duce, as loudly as he could, in the conviction that
those black-shirted fanatics would become furious enough
to lynch him on the spot. But the poor man was oddly dis-
appointed; the more he cried out, the less the fascists paid
him any attention. Only after a long time and many efforts
did an officer come out of the ranks to whisper anxiously
in his ear: "Beware! Down there, at the end of the column,
is a chap who really believes in fascism. Don't let yourself
be heard by him, if you don't want to get into trouble!"
When man's freedom is curbed by terrorism, be it by either
a Mussolini or the Holy Office, the result is always the
same, and similarly mixed up with tragedy and farce.

Moreover, things are not made better for us by the fact
that Galileo was neither suspected by the Church before
1612, when the Dominicans of Florence started their cam-
paign against him, nor did he write on topics connected
with religion before his letters to Castelli in 1613 and to
Christine of Lorraine in 1615. In other words, our main
sources of information about his attitude toward Christianity concern only the last part of his life, from his forty-
eighth year onward. A man in his fifties has an already
consolidated body of opinions, formed through long years
of experience, reflection, and study, the value of which can

be appreciated only in the light of their entire growth process. But our information is exasperatingly scarce on Galileo's experience and thought on religion before 1612. His biographers, such as Vincenzio Galilei, Viviani, and Gherardini are silent on this topic; his works and correspondence give us but scant or uncertain data; the documents that the modern erudites have gathered about him are not much richer. We are compelled to resort to conjectures, however reluctant one can be to advance on so slippery a ground.

Perhaps one of the few sure pieces of data we can rely upon is the fact that Galileo was a child of the Galilei family of Florence. That is not a joke, nor a Lapalissian truth by any means. A Galilei, in sixteenth-century Florence, was not unlike a Norton or a Prescott, if not a Winthrop or an Adams, in later centuries in New England. A Bostonian Brahmin belonged to a well-defined social, cultural, and even religious environment by birth. A Renaissance Florentine was not less conditioned by his birth, if he was the scion of a family of *cittadini*. From this point of view, the fact that Galileo was actually born in Pisa and resided there or in Padua for many years was irrelevant. Not all the people who were born or dwelled within the city walls were citizens of Florence, but only those whose families had given members to the city government in the past. Practically speaking, that was the same as being members of the Arti, and possibly of the Arti Maggiori, which controlled the most lucrative trades and professions. Inversely, all the scions of these families were cittadini, regardless of their place of birth and of their residence. In her golden age, Florence was not unlike a modern corporation, whose cittadini were the shareholders by hereditary right. And that had a deciding influence not only in social status, but also in professional orientation. A striking evidence of that is offered by Galileo's own family. Its fortune was made mostly by a Galileo Galilei (1370?–1450?) who served a term as *gonfaloniere di giustizia* and was a successful physician, that is, a member of the Arte dei Medici e Speziali, one of the Arti Maggiori to which Dante belonged in his time. When our Galileo was born, the old gonfaloniere had been in his grave for more than a century and Florence had ceased to be a republic since 1530. By that time, many a family of cittadini, including the Galilei, felt sorely the effects of the economic crisis brought about by the wars and the inflation of the American silver. However, Galileo's father Vincenzio was still a merchant, as was becoming to a descendant of cittadini, although he was prominent also as a musician. He gave his son the same name as the gonfaloniere and tried to put him in the same medical profession, after a first vain attempt—if we are to believe the doubtful witness of Gherardini—to make a wool-trader out of him. Probably Galileo was a bit of a rebel, when he put aside medicine for mathematics. But he clung to family traditions enough to call his own son Vincenzio; this son tried to find a living in a bureaucratic career but finally became a chancellor of the Arte dei Mercatanti. Incidentally, in his time, Galileo the gonfaloniere owned a villa in the Arcetri Hill, where Galileo the scientist was to put his daughters in a convent and spend the last years of his life.

Family tradition was influential also in ethics, religion, and intellectual life. A cittadino felt that he had a hereditary share in Florence's moral, intellectual, and artistic treasure, as well as in her wealth. He paid homage to the great Trecento writers, Dante, Petrarch, and Boccaccio, as to a kind of household god; in particular he worshiped the "altissimo poeta," whose *Divine Comedy* was supposed to be full of high moral and philosophical truth, along with its superhuman beauty. He considered as part of his heritage the masterpieces with which Florence had been filled

by an uninterrupted chain of geniuses from Giotto to
Michelangelo. But, here again, beauty and truth coincided,
since the Florence cittadino was convinced that the works
of the great artists had a lofty philosophical and religious
message for those spirits who could go beyond exterior appearances. The "divino Michelangelo," in particular, was
not less great as a "moral philosopher" and a Christian
than he was as an artist. Many a cittadino had a spiritual
share also in the treasure of the sanctity and martyrdom of
Savonarola or in that of the idealism of the Neoplatonic
philosophers; many more had a share in the treasure of
classical learning accumulated by the Florentine humanists.
But each cittadino was sure that he had at least a share in
the *volgare,* the most perfect jewel of Florence's spiritual
crown, which the other Italians could only labor to imi-
tate, but could never possess.

Each of these privileges had its counterpart in a duty.
A cittadino was aware that he was given so many gifts not
so much as an individual, part of the city community, but
rather as a part of a series of communities such as Florence,
and possibily a determined quarter of the city; or a well-
determined social group; or a family group. He felt himself belonging to these communities in the fullest sense of
the word. He was expected to serve in the various public
offices when his turn came; he was to embrace a profession
or a trade becoming to his status; he was to lead the kind
of active, useful, and responsible life that the Florence
Humanists had described in their treatises; he was to live
up to his artistic, intellectual, and moral heritage. Above
all, he was to be a dedicated member of his family, ready
to sacrifice his own tastes or interests to the family's honor,
wealth, and continuity. He was to respect in his father the
visible symbol of the family and to obey him even as an
adult. All these duties were not so much prescribed by
men's written laws as imposed on the cittadino's conscience

by God's own law: Christianity was the same with family and city, with morals and art, with father Dante and one's own father, with Michelangelo's *David* and the duty of caring for the poor and the hospitals. All this was the cornerstone of the solid moral universe of the Florence cittadino.

In fact, the cittadini's God was not unlike a solid businessman: he paid everyone his due in this life or after, and expected to be given sound facts of charity and righteousness and not to be cheated by empty words. Therefore, conscience did not play a lesser role in old Florence than it was to play in a later age among the Puritans. After all, much of the Puritan doctrine was drawn from the teaching of a Florentine, Peter Martys Vermigli. But that did not imply a sheepish attitude toward God's ministers: on the contrary, priests and friars were not held particularly high in the cittadini's opinion. A Florence cittadino knew too well the mocking stories about faked miracles and impudent friars circulated by Boccaccio or the strong words used by Dante and Petrarch to brand the vices of the clergy. In a sense, a bit of anticlericalism was as necessary as a sound amount of the fear of God to a really respectable cittadino and a good Christian.

However, when Galileo was born, the formerly coherent and solid Florentine moral universe was disintegrating. Florence was no more a republic, and the Medici *signoria* was now a *principato,* whose grand dukes modeled themselves on the pattern of the absolute kings of their times. As bureaucracy replaced the formerly honorary offices, so a dull conformity to the will of the *superiori* replaced the old sense of public responsibility. But a king of Spain or of France was clearly such by divine right, while God could hardly be invoked to justify a Medici's rule. The members of the former ruling class called themselves *nobili* instead of cittadini and addressed each other as *signore,* instead of *messere,* as their more austere ancestors did. But it was not a matter of words only. The economic crisis discouraged the traditional business activities, as it encouraged an idler and more lavish way of life. It was not so sure anymore that God required an active, conscientious, and relatively parsimonious life. Artists and poets were no more supposed to have lofty messages of religious and human idealism; they were to offer a purely aesthetic delight or to be the instruments of Church and state propaganda. A frightened silence replaced the traditional Florentine taste for political and ideological discussion. Apparently religion was untouched by the crisis of the old political, social, and economic ways of life. Articles of faith and acts of worship were more or less the same as in the days of Dante and Savonarola, although they had lost much of their former meaning. Christianity had been too tightly associated with the old order of things to survive as more than an empty shell.

The shell was even harder than it used to be. The Counter-Reformation had stressed the institutional aspects of the Church and increased its power of repression. The clergy could impose its influence far more effectively than before, and obtained by terror what it had never obtained previously by consent. Few if any dared to defy this overwhelming machinery of power, and those who did paid dearly for it. As in all totalitarian regimes, propaganda and brain-washing could get spectacular effects; they could stampede the mobs into near-frenzied emotions and give all the appearances of an impressive unanimity of consent. But in several instances compulsory unanimity hardly masked the creeping skepticism. At any rate, the old unity was lost; a layman knew he had to leave religious policy to the care of the Church's superiori just as a citizen knew he had to leave politics to the care of the state's superiori. Equally, an artist knew he had to content himself with being an expert on beautiful form, and a scholar knew he had to let certain sleeping dogs lie, if he did not want to get himself into trouble.

We have significant evidence of the spiritual crisis the late sixteenth-century Florentines underwent, which ranges from Michelangelo's madness in his last works of art and poems to Doni's nervous restlessness. Another interesting, if less known, item of evidence of the same thing is Bastiano Arditi's diary, the journal of an old and pious cittadino, who wrote when Galileo was a boy, under Grand Duke Francesco I. Arditi was as saddened by Florence's economic decadence as by Francesco's ruthless absolutism and dissipated way of life, and he still considered that politics, morals, and economics were one with Christianity, so much so that the decadence of the one appeared to him as the decadence also of the other. Galileo was born too late to feel the same pangs of conscience; however, the Galilei were close friends of the Buonarroti. Moreover, his tremendous vitality and joie de vivre made him temperamentally impenetrable to melancholy. But he was enough a man of his times to bear the marks of the disintegration of the old unity.

It is almost superfluous to emphasize how much in Galileo's personality corresponded still to the portrait of the Florence cittadino: his manly realism, his love of an active life, and of anything useful and concretely practical; his typically Florentine irony and his high opinion and masterly use of the volgare; his enthusiasm for poetry, music, fine arts in general, and for Dante and Michelangelo in particular; his strong humanistic background, his fondness for Plato, and his exalted conception of man's intellectual dignity, so near to that of the fifteenth-century Florentine Neoplatonists. Galileo's dedication to his family was not less typical. A respectful child of his father, Vincenzio, as long as the latter lived, Galileo underwent the heaviest financial sacrifices after his father's death to supply his sisters with appropriate dowries and to help his irresponsible and luckless brother Michelangelo. (Incidentally, it is interesting to note how, in his letters to Galileo, Michelangelo insisted on couching his requests for help in religious terms: God in person requested that Galileo support his unpecunious brother.) And Galileo eventually let himself be plundered by his not-always-deserving or grateful family all through his life. Perhaps his celibacy was also an effect of his sense of family responsibility. He spent so much to marry off his sisters that he did not have enough money for himself, to set up a home, when the time was opportune.

But, on the other hand, Galileo's private life had little in common with the parsimonious austerity of the former generations' cittadini. One has but to compare the ribald verses of Galileo's poem "Contro il portare la toga" with Michelangelo's love poetry, so filled with lofty Neoplatonic idealism, or Michelangelo's thrifty investments of his earnings with Galileo's endless struggles against debt and casual handling of money to grasp the difference between the two ages. It is possible that Galileo left his Venetian mistress, Marina Gamba, when he decided to move back from Padua to Florence, in deference to the morals of his native environment. The Florence cittadini not infrequently had natural children with a house servant or with a *contadina*, but public opinion frowned upon Cosimo I and Francesco I when they had steady relations with a kind of official mistress. But Galileo's private life did not become more puritanical for that, if we are to judge from the fact that he could be exhorted to set aside his "disorders" even in his old age, and even by so worldly a friend as Sagredo. Anyhow, the important fact is that love did not exist for him except in the physical sense of the word. There was no Beatrice, Laura, or Vittoria Colonna to give love the same idealistic meaning that it had for Dante, Petrarch, and Michelangelo. Physical love was in a compartment of its own, without relation to the rest of Galileo's life.

Even as a fervent lover of music and the fine arts, Galileo never tried to draw a moral, philosophical, or religious message from them. In his notes on Ariosto and Tasso he showed himself to be a penetrating and gifted literary critic, but his criticism was exclusively literary. It did not allow any room for ideological issues. In his youth, he paid his tribute to Dante's worship in the form of an essay, on the topography of the *Inferno*, which is a little masterpiece of logic, technical skill, and volgare prose. But it does not reveal any particular commitment to Dante's ideals. The reader cannot even detect whether Galileo was convinced that an "Inferno" existed. There is some indication that Galileo had Savonarola's writings among his not-many books, but there is no evidence that they had any influence upon him. Joachim of Flori's prophesies could have but an ironic mention in the *Dialogo dei massimi sistemi*. The strong eschatological tension which was so evident in Dante, Savonarola, and Michelangelo, was foreign to Galileo's mind. Poetry and art were just as disarticulated from their traditional ideological context. They had to find their reason for existing in themselves only.

According to all evidence, there was still a strong vein of Florentine patriotism in Galileo. Since the "nazione e città di Firenze" was now identified with the house of the Medici, it is probable that he was reasonably sincere when he professed his loyalty to the grand dukes. But Galileo's letters are silent on anything concerning politics. A reader could go through all of them without realizing that he lived in an age of terrific European convulsions, corresponding to most of the Thirty Years War. Politics and government were no longer integral parts of the general problem of man's destiny upon this earth, as they had been for Dante and Savonarola, Machiavelli and Michelangelo. They were a technical department of their own, to be left to the care of authorized experts. Whether Galileo was happy or unhappy with that is anyone's guess. The fact is that he did not let himself become entangled in problems of that kind, either by willful choice or by sheer prudence. In a hopelessly fragmented world each man was to choose his compartment to live in and his goal to live for. Galileo had no doubt that his life's raison d'etre was in his activities as a "mathematician" and as a "natural philosopher," to put it in the words of his times. The rest was relatively unimportant to him; or, rather, it could only be instrumental to the achievement of his goal—*all* the rest, including madonna Marina, of course.

On the other hand, the historical environment in which Galileo lived did not provide him with a foundation upon which to build anew. As we will see later, in his investigation of the natural universe a religious element was not foreign. But his fight for truth had little in common with the conflicts that his contemporaries considered religious: Catholicism versus Protestantism; curialism versus anticurialism; orthodoxy versus hereticism—or "libertinism," as Campanella called it in his *Atheismus triumphatus*. In his adolescence, Galileo was the pupil of a Vallombrosa monk and probably was also a novice in a convent of that order. (From Vincenzio Galilei's correspondence with his friend Muzio Tedaldi, Antonio Favaro deduced that the latter congratulated himself, along with Galileo's father, when the adolescent came back from the Vallombrosa friars. Evidently, although a man of rigid morality, Vincenzio was not an enthusiast of having a male child distracted from active life by the monks' influence. And that is well in line with a typical attitude of the old Florence cittadini; they seldom considered a call to monastic life as a blessing, except for women, and then only to save the family the expense of paying dowries.) Anyhow, Galileo's experience among the monks was short and negative. If we are to believe in Viviani's witness, it left him but a sense of boredom for the dry formalism of the scholastics he had been introduced to. Soon after, Galileo had a diametrically opposite experience, that of the heterodox interpretation of Aristotle, in the line of the Averroist and Alexandrist tradition. It was not short, but it did not fare better than his initiation into the orthodox Aristotelism of the scholastics.

Galileo's biographers have oddly underrated the fact that often the champions of the Aristotelism against which he battled all through his life were not religious people at all. It is too simple indeed to present Galileo's battle for truth as only a battle for intellectual freedom against the dogmatism of the Church. In a way, also, many an opponent of Galileo, such as Cremonini, was fighting for his intellectual freedom to dissent from Catholic orthodoxy. Galileo did not live in a world of blind fundamentalists; he lived when a radical naturalism was largely creeping into Italy's universities. However, it was compelled to mask itself under an unintelligible Latin jargon for fear of the Inquisition. Then, if ever, Italy was notorious as a hotbed of hereticism and atheism beyond the Alps. To put it in its simplest form, this radical naturalism or "libertinism" held that Nature—uncreated and everlasting—was the only true reality. Obviously its main targets were the doctrines of the world's creation by a transcendent God and of the immortality of man's soul, together with revealed religions such as Judaism, Christianity, and Islam. According to the libertines, Moses, Jesus, and Mohammed were impostors, who fascinated the ignorant mobs with pretended miracles in order to have them submit to their laws. But miracles were only apparent; any wise man, instructed in the secrets of natural laws, could repeat them by the force of natural magic. Man was merely a natural phenomenon, whose destiny was fixed by Nature with iron determinism. However, although connected mostly with Averroism or Alexandrism, libertinism could be associated also with other philosophies, as with Bruno, or with the early stage of Campanella's philosophy, before his conversion to Christianity in his Neapolitan jail. Even more often, it was associated with the idea that stars had a predominant influence in determining man's life. At a certain conjunction of stars, a lawgiver would appear to begin the cycle of a religion, until a new conjunction would bring it to its end. Bruno was convinced that the cycle of Christianity was at its end and he was to be the new lawgiver of the coming new age. A similar conviction led Campanella to start his unlucky conspiracy against the Spaniards in the year 1600. These doctrines can appear to us as dreams of exalted minds, but they appeared as based upon positive science to seventeenth-century men—and their influence was not always confined to academic circles.

Of Girolamo Borri, a prominent member of the Pisa faculty when Galileo was there as a student, Gabriel Naudé wrote:

> C'étoiet un athée parfait; il n'a pas été brulé, mais il le méritoit bien. Il avoit dit un jour que *supra octavam sphaeram nihil est*. Le inquisiteur le voulût obliger de se dédire. Il monta en chaire le lendemain et dit à ses auditeurs: 'Messieurs, je vous ai maintenu et prouvé que *supra octavam sphaeram nihil est;* on veut que je me dédise; je vous assure que s'il y a autre chose, ce ne peut être qu'un plât de macaroni pour M. l'inquisiteur.' *Quo dicto, se fuga proripiens saluti consuluit.* Il eût été brulé plusieurs fois sans le Grand-Duc qui l'aimoit.

Cremonini was not less known as an atheist and the Inquisition tried to open a trial against him more than once. However, he could live peacefully in Padua, thanks to the protection of the Venetian nobility. A theory of religion as a law to curb the otherwise unruly mob was not unpleasant to the ears of an absolute prince or of an oligarchy, provided it was cautiously wrapped in technical terms, unintelligible to most. Even a pope, such as Urban VIII, was notorious for his fondness of astrologers.

These scholars, who labeled Galileo a forerunner of the eighteenth-century Enlightenment and of modern secularism, have probably underrated the fact that the first mentioned adopted largely the libertine theory of religion and the second stems from some kind of immanentism. During his life, Galileo did come into contact with immanentistic currents of thought, whose corollary was a theory of religion as the work of imposture, but he was far from showing any sympathy for them. Among Galileo's earliest papers, there are notes of the lectures in natural philosophy that he heard in Pisa, in 1584. These contain ample discussion of whether the world is eternal or was created by God. They are an interesting evidence of the kind of problems that Galileo could be initiated into at Pisa. But they conclude in favor of the orthodox doctrine. When he was a lecturer in Pisa in the *Capitolo contro il portare la toga,* Galileo humorously presented nakedness as the natural condition of men and women, and dresses as a nuisance to which one had to be resigned in the name of God. Such a statement smells suspiciously of the libertine's criticism of the revealed religions and morals, and of their revindication of the natural instincts. However, the *Capitolo* is evidently mocking: Galileo showed in it that he was aware of the radical naturalism of his heterodox colleagues, but he did not take it seriously. In the years he spent in Padua, he had Cremonini among his fellow professors, and in a later period of his life he had to defend his theories against Fortunio Liceti and Antonio Rocco. Both Liceti and Rocco were members of the Venetian Academy of the Incogniti, which was a notorious nest of libertines. Rocco in particular has been detected by modern scholars as being the

author of *Alcibiade fanciullo a scuola,* a peppery anonymous pamphlet in which the theory of morals and religions
as the work of impostors is openly embraced. But it is well
known how little respect was accorded by Galileo to Cremonini's blind faith in Aristotle, or how cordially he de-
spised Rocco as an "ignorantissimo bue." And it is superfluous to say how Liceti's opportunistic treatment of the
problem of the soul's immortality was stamped with corro-
sive irony in the *Dialogo dei massimi sistemi.*

In an age in which a zealous bigotry could be an excel-
lent means of disposing of one's detractors, it is striking
that Galileo never fell into the temptation of silencing any
peripatetic adversary by denouncing him as a heretic. It
is an admirable instance of fair play and of moral integrity,
as well as evidence of Galileo's strenuous will of keeping
scientific discussion quite apart from Church matters. But
it is also evidence that Galileo's fight for truth was a battle
on two fronts, against both the scholastic and the heterodox
interpretation of Aristotle.

Galileo's experience was quite different in the instance
of the Venetian anticurialists with whom he associated
when he was at Padua. Sarpi and Micanzio and their patrician friends such as Sagredo, Morosini, and Niccolò Con-
tarini were a permanent source of strength and inspiration
to him throughout his life. These men did not consider
science as a compartment of its own, isolated from the rest
of human activities; it was part of a coherent moral world
to which they felt earnestly committed as citizens and
scholars, as men bound by duties toward God and their
families or friends, and as parts of the collective destiny
of the Serenissima republic. Of course, Sarpi's and Mic
zio's crypto-Protestantism was not the same thing as their
patrician friends' royalist Catholicism or Sagredo's mocking anticlericalism; Morosini's austere moralism and Sarpi's
asceticism were not the same thing as Sagredo's worldly

wisdom. But all these men felt that the advancement of learning was one with Venice's struggle for her political freedom against Spain and for her spiritual independence against the Roman Curia and the Jesuits, and that created a strong enough common ground to bind them by a link of affectionate solidarity, as partners in the same enterprise.

Despite Galileo's customary prudence in his writings, these last examples offer indications that he shared the traditional attitude of the Florentine forefathers toward priests and friars. He could not be scandalized by his Venetian friends' attitudes. He made use of their contacts with the Protestant world to penetrate spiritually beyond the iron curtain of the Counter-Reformation. He was more than likely close to the ideological positions of the Sarpi circle. One of the few mentions of current affairs in Galileo's correspondence concerns the expulsion of the Jesuits from Venice in 1606, upon which he commented in clearly ironic terms in a letter to his brother Michelangelo. Other significant evidence can be drawn from Galileo's correspondence with Martin Hastal. In a letter from Prague in 1610 Hastal begged him to warn Sarpi that his clandestine correspondence with Badovere in France had been detected by his enemies. This is a good indication that Galileo was a party to Sarpi's secrets. Another letter by Hastal warned Galileo himself that the Spaniards were incensed against his *Sidereus nuncius* because it was a danger to the Catholic cause. And it is a pity that we have but Hastal's letters; probably Galileo's letters to Hastal would offer many another interesting indication. Anyhow, Galileo's friendship with Sarpi was suspicious enough to be used against him by Father Caccini in a deposition at the Holy Office in 1615.

However, Galileo did not ever fully identify his scientific mission with his Venetian friends' cause. To explain his departure from Padua he wrote that Venice would

never let him attend to scientific work only, relieving him
of other duties, because a republic ought to be responsible
to the public for the use of money, while a despotic prince
could spend freely and could afford for himself a full time
scientist in his pay. Sagredo was more than justified in
objecting to him that he would not find the same "libertà e
monarchia di se stesso" as he had found in Venice and to
warn him against the risks to which he was going to be
exposed in Florence. And modern scholars have often criti-
cized Galileo's imprudence and his naïveté in his unhappy
dealings with the Church, in which he found himself involved soon after his coming back to Florence. But I am
not sure that imprudence and naïveté are sufficient to explain Galileo's behavior in the crucial years of his life, from
his departure from Padua in 1610 to his condemnation by
the Roman Inquisition. Obviously, his exuberant tempera-
ment had a strong part in his overoptimistic confidence in
the success of his scientific mission, which proved itself
fatal to him. But in the light of Galileo's letters to Castelli,
Dini, and Christine of Lorraine, and of his *Dialogo dei
massimi sistemi,* one is led to think that his indomitable
optimism also had its roots in convictions that had taken
the shape of a religious creed. Unfortunately, we cannot be
sure whether the creed Galileo exposed in the above-
mentioned writings existed in him already at the time when
he came back to Florence, or whether he reached these
conclusions only later, under the challenge of adversity.
Strictly speaking, we cannot be sure even whether that
creed expressed Galileo's mind fully or whether he still con-
cealed a part of his thoughts on religion. However, we cannot reasonably doubt that Galileo's quest for truth had
taken the shape of a fight for true science against the false
science of the Peripatetics. Inevitably, his fight for truth
against falsehood assumed the character of a crusade for
Good against Evil. He could not doubt the final victory of

the one over the other without putting in doubt all the conclusions he had reached after a whole life.

Probably Galileo was rendered somewhat immune to radical naturalism by his Florentine heritage. From the time of Petrarch's polemic against the Averroists in his *De sui ipsius et multorum ignorantia* a long ideological war had raged, in which Christianity and humanism had been allied against astrology and Alexandrism or Averroism, and Florence had played an important role in this struggle through her Neoplatonic humanists, such as Pico della Mirandola and Savonarola. However, the pantheistic mysticism of the Neoplatonics, as well as Savonarola's eschatological prophesies, had little attraction for Galileo's lucid mind. Therefore, Galileo's God was nearer to Plato's Demiourgos than to the Neoplatonic World Soul, not to speak of Aristotle's Motionless Motor. But Galileo went as far as to discuss—in a fascinating page of the *Dialogo dei massimi sistemi*—the hypothesis that the planets could have been pushed by God into their present places with a linear movement and then they could have started their present circular movements. Such a hypothesis presumes evidently that the work of the world's divine artificer was not limited to the creation; it allows the possibility of God's intervention to shape the universe even after its creation, or, better, an infinite possibility of interventions. In his letter to Christine of Lorraine Galileo affirmed that his Copernican system was more compatible than the Ptolemaic one with the Scripture story according to which God stopped the sun at Joshua's request. It is possible that he was simply trying to defend himself as best he could; but it is also possible that he was entirely sincere. In his thought, as it is exposed in his main writings on religion, there is nothing repugnant to an intervention by God such as in Joshua's story. There is only an all out repugnance to identifying God with immobility and inaction.

Galileo's epistemology was also influenced by Plato's theory of inborn ideas, in its basic inspiration. Man has to set aside the bookish science of the Peripatetics to read directly in the great book of Nature, which is written by its Creator in mathematical characters. But in reading this book, man does not do anything else than discover a truth already hidden in his mind. Also, Simplicio would be able to reach the truth, if only he would leave aside his Aristotelean prejudices and let himself be guided by Sagredo's questions, since the Simplicios are also men and therefore endowed with the divine gift of knowledge. Man's science is inferior to God's, because man can reach but a part of the truth, while God knows it all. The one needs a long labor to arrive at his limited truth, while the other has it intuitively. But intrinsically man's knowledge is not of another quality than God's. And man's intellectual potential is so great because it precedes, in a certain sense, humanity itself. The spark of knowledge is so bright, because it burns with God's own light. Galileo's man is no longer a passive tool of blind natural forces, as he was in the libertine's view. He has been reinstated in his full dignity as the exceptional creature, similar to God—but he is now so high because God is no more a Motionless Motor but has also been reinstated in the full majesty of His transcendent omnipotence.

The problem is now whether such a doctrine is to be identified with Christianity. Galileo's philosophy is a fascinating *theologia gloriae,* but it is far from being a *theologia crucis.* Jesus Christ fits nowhere in it, and, in fact, his name seldom if ever appears under Galileo's pen. Galileo could have answered that the problem of redemption was not in the scientist's province and that he willingly left it to the cares of the professional theologians. When he put Nature's book side by side with the Bible, as the twin means of knowledge offered by God to man, he was probably sincere. But the fact remains that his consideration of man was exclusively *sub specie scientiae,* outside the Christian dialectic of fall and redemption. He would only laugh at the endless discussions of the Peripatetics about the soul's mortality or immortality; since man's mind participated in God's science, it was simply foolish to discuss whether or not it participated also in God's eternity. Galileo was sure that man would be given by God an entire knowledge of truth after his death, instead of the partial knowledge granted to him on the earth. But he again put the accent upon knowledge; and Christianity cannot be reduced to a problem of epistemology.

Of course, a long tradition tended to identify Platonism with Christianity and Galileo could be convinced in good faith that his philosophy was Christian. His conscience was never torn by a conflict between faith and science: materially he was a victim of such a conflict, because the Church decided that his scientific findings were in conflict with Catholic dogmas, but spiritually he was the least troubled of men, so much was he convinced that no conflict existed. All through the long ordeal of his dealings with the Holy Office, he never admitted that there was any ideological problem at stake. He stubbornly insisted that there was merely a pragmatic problem, to be solved diplomatically, mainly through the political influence of the Tuscan court and a good bit of lobbying in Rome's most influential circles.

Modern scholars are probably right when they state that Galileo should have realized that his philosophy could not be tolerated by the Church, since it went against the very foundations of the authoritarian and reactionary system of the Counter-Reformation. However, it is a fact that Galileo did not even suspect that such a conflict would arise. The Church had made of itself a mighty machinery of power. He took it as such and was ready to negotiate with it in pragmatic terms, which are the only sensible ones when one has to deal with a power. In a departmental-ized world, he had kept himself scrupulously in his own scientific compartment; he did not try to defy the Roman Curia, as Sarpi had done, at the risk of being stabbed by its killers. His conscience was quiet. Even when he was con-demned by the Holy Office, no pangs of conscience and no terror of damnation assailed him. His dramatic relations with the Church were never a religious drama for him.

To the end of his days, he maintained his conviction that he had been the victim of his enemies' intrigues and ill will. Of course he was wrong: he did not realize that a basic conflict did exist between the spirit of immobility of the Counter-Reformation and his philosophy which iden-tified immobility with evil. But it is probable that he was not wrong for an excess of naïveté, but for an excess of realism. He so much considered the Church as a power machine that he almost forgot it was also a religious insti-tution with an ideological sensitivity of its own. And the fact that those in his Florentine environment thought ex-actly like him does not diminish Galileo's error. When Gali-leo underwent his first ordeal in Rome in 1616, the letters of Picchena and Guicciardini, respectively the Florence court's prime minister and its ambassador in Rome, prove that they were convinced that Galileo's only wrong was his delusion that the Roman courtiers and the friars could behave as enlightened or simply sensible people. They never took seriously the idea that a problem of faith was in-volved in the matter. "Vostra signoria," wrote Picchena to him, "che ha assaggiato le persecuzioni fratine, sa di che sapore elle sono .... e i frati sono omnipotenti." And Pic-chena's realistic language was mild in comparison with that of Father Caccini's own brother, who branded the cam-paign against Galileo as a "fratata," "a friars' prowess," making it an equivalent of impudence and wickedness. We cannot reproach Galileo too severely because he did not realize what nobody around him realized, that is, that his trial went much beyond the limits of a "fratata."

Incidentally, one should also consider the peculiar relations existing between Florence and Rome in Galileo's times. A long series of popes, born either in Florence or in her domain, or at least connected with the grand duchy in one way or another—Leo X, Clement VII, Julius III, Marcellus II, Pius IV, Clement VIII, Leo XI, Paul V, Urban VIII, soon to be followed by Alexander VII and Clement IX—had made of Rome a kind of colony to be exploited by powerful Etruscan clans. Saints such as Roberto Bellarmino and Filippo Neri emerged also among the Tuscan immigrants in Rome. But sanctity was not abundant even in the sixteenth and seventeenth centuries. Opportunism and profit had a far stronger appeal to the fortune-seekers who came from Florence to Rome than did piety or zeal. As a Florentine, Galileo had some justification at least in his conviction that lobbying and diplomacy could get anything in Rome.

As a matter of fact, Galileo's drama was in good part a family quarrel among Florentines. His 1616 trial was originated by fathers Lorini and Caccini and was decided by Roberto Bellarmino, of Montepulciano, under Paul V of Siena. And, since it was handled by a man such as Bellarmino, on whose professional integrity as a heretic-hunter no doubt is possible, it had a relatively mild conclusion. But the second trial was even more clearly a family affair, as it had a whole group of Florentines among its protagonists; Pope Urban VIII and his Barberini nephews, Father Riccardi, Father Firenzuola, Monsignore Ciampoli, and the ambassador Niccolini. It was far more influenced by the uneasy course of the relations between metropolis and colony and by piques of religious orders than by genuinely religious preoccupations. And it fared far worse than the first for Galileo. To call Galileo's condemnation an act of fanatical intolerance is to pay undue homage to its protagonist's character. Nor did the non-Florentines who had a hand in it behave more idealistically. At least one of the judges who sat in Galileo's condemnation—Cardinal Bentivoglio—has left us his autobiography. However dull, it is a meaningful document. It is the candid confession of a careerist who looked at the Church as only a ladder, whose rungs were to be climbed by shrewdness and maneuvering skill. Nowhere in this book can one find a word of faith and piety. The Roman Jesuits who did so much to bring Galileo to ruin were probably the first to know that he was scientifically right. Anyhow, their spokesman at the tribunal was Father Melchior Inchofer, who is strongly suspected of being the author of *Monarchia solissorum,* one of the most diffused clandestine pamphlets of the seventeenth century and a vitriolic satire of the Jesuits' greed for power. Probably the same man who posed as the champion of the Jesuits' line ridiculed it behind the backs of his fellow Jesuits. Poor Galileo was not so unjustified in his purely pragmatic approach to the problem of his relations with the Church.

However, it is not impossible that a certain religious element was present also in this depressing environment. Galileo hoped against all reasonable forecast that men would yield in the end to truth, however ill disposed or unworthy. This attitude appears so much in contradiction to reality that one is led to think that it was inspired by faith more than by anything else. Possibly Galileo could not resign himself to admit that truth would not prevail, because in that case he would have to admit that God, the divine artificer, was impotent. He refused to the last to believe that his fellowmen would not listen to him, because he could not despair of them without despairing of their Creator. That is a mere conjecture, of course. But it is not to be lightly excluded. Perhaps Galileo's trial is the best evidence of the depth of his religiousness.

IV

THE PROBLEM OF FORCE
IN GALILEO'S PHYSICS

Richard S. Westfall

*O*BVIOUS perils are involved when a Newtonian scholar is invited to a conference on Galileo. He is apt to confuse the two ends of the seventeenth century and to employ the achievement of Newton as a criterion by which to measure that of Galileo. Such proceedings would constitute a public scandal at the celebration of the 400th anniversary of Galileo's birth, and I feel obliged to protest my innocence by placing the blame on those who planned the program—I mean my gracious hosts who have so kindly paid my expenses to come all this way. I have problems enough without shouldering the blame; the Newtonian scholar who dares to discuss Galileo in the presence of Giorgio de Santillana is obviously in greater danger than ever Galileo was.

Galileo's writings present a paradox to one who examines them from the perspective of the later seventeenth century and especially of Newton, and who attempts to define Galileo's concept of force. He recognizes at once familiar landmarks on the intellectual terrain. The concept of inertia, however imperfectly formulated, has recast the problem of force in a new mold. If I may alter a sentence from Descartes, from now on the question will be, not what keeps a body in motion, but what changes its state of motion or rest. He nods in agreement when Galileo declares that a body on a horizontal plane "finds itself in a condition of indifference as to motion or rest; has no inherent tendency to move in any direction, and offers no resistance to being set in motion." [1] And he nods the more as Galileo moves on from this premise to discuss the "nonoperative quality of motion among the things which share it in common," so that such motion is "insensible, imperceptible, and without any effect whatever." [2] Because of the indifference of matter, the same body can participate in more motions than one; each motion proceeds unhampered, and the result reveals itself by means of the familiar parallelogram. Manifestly we stand in the presence of the lifeless mechanical matter of seventeenth-century science. Dead and inert, stripped of the Aristotelian natures that were their principles of motion, bodies rest in their state of indifference, wholly submissive to whatever impulse may impinge upon them.

If the concept of inertia dominates the landscape, other familiar sights crowd about it. Galileo denies at once the homocentricity of medieval cosmology, according to which the whole universe exists for the benefit of man, and also the uniqueness of the earth or of any other body as a

[1] Galileo, *Dialogues Concerning Two New Sciences,* trans. by Henry Crew and Alfonso de Salvio (New York, 1914), p. 181. I shall cite this work hereafter by its proper name, *Discourses.* The words quoted here are from the pen of Viviani, but they are written at Galileo's suggestion and embody his thought. Cf. Galileo's remark in *Mechanics:* a body on a horizontal plane will remain at rest "though with a disposition to be moved by any extremely small force." (*On Motion and On Mechanics,* trans. and ed. by I. E. Drabkin and Stillman Drake [Madison, 1960], p. 170.) Cf. also, the sixth day of the *Discourses:* ". . . there is no resistance (except an infinite one) that is able to resist a blow without moving . . ." (*Le opere di Galileo Galilei,* ed. by Antonio Favaro, ed. nazionale, 20 vols. in 21 [Firenze, 1890–1909], VIII, 337.)

[2] Galileo, *Dialogue Concerning the Two Chief World Systems— Ptolemaic and Copernican,* trans. by Stillman Drake (Berkeley and Los Angeles, 1953), p. 171.

center in the cosmos. Equally he affirms the homogeneity of matter. All bodies are composed of the same stuff, the inert matter indifferent to motion, its particles more or less closely packed together. All bodies then are heavy; all are subject to identical laws of motion. Generation and corruption, the most fundamental changes in Aristotelian science, are nothing more than "a simple transposition of parts. . . ." [3] The famous passage in the *Assayer* appears to assert, in its denial of the reality of secondary qualities, that physical nature is composed solely of the particles of inert matter. "I do not believe," Galileo states, "that for exciting in us tastes, odors, and sounds there are required in external bodies anything but sizes, shapes, numbers, and slow or fast movements; and I think that if ears, tongues, and noses were taken away, shapes and numbers and motions would remain but not odors or tastes or sounds." [4] All this is well-known country to one who frequents the later seventeenth century, and he looks about expectantly for that creature who comes to inhabit it and by inhabiting it to make it intelligible. I mean the concept of force which historically provides the ultimate key to reading the language of mathematics in which the mechanical world we are describing expresses itself—the language Galileo wants so much to read. I say he "looks" for the concept of force, although more than one historian of science has not paused long enough to look, but, moved by the logic of the situation, has simply asserted that it is there. The paradox that I spoke of for the Newtonian scholar consists precisely in the fact that the concept of force, so obviously demanded by the context, is not there.

It is not the question of terminology that concerns me. Certainly the word *forza* appears in Galileo's physics. Part

[3] *Ibid.*, p. 40.
[4] *The Controversy on the Comets of 1618,* trans. by Stillman Drake and C. D. O'Malley (Philadelphia, 1960), p. 311.

of the problem lies in the very abundance of its presence. If we can legitimately translate it by "force" in many instances, in an equal number we cannot.[5] Other words, al-

[5] Since "force" (*forza*) is the term that has come to designate that which changes a body's state of rest or motion, more than a little interest attaches to Galileo's use of the word. Easily his most consistent usage occurs in discussions of simple machines; the *forza* applied to one end of the lever (Galileo reduces all simple machines to the lever) balances and overcomes the resistance at the other end. (Cf. *Discourses*, pp. 110–115, 137–138; *Mechanics*, p. 158. Although I quote from English translations, I have checked these instances and all those in which I cite the Italian word in the *Opere*.) Since Galileo's analysis of percussion rests on its analogy to the lever, also, the phrase *forza della percossa* is a natural extension of this usage; the velocity of a moving body multiplies its weight just as levers and screws multiply the *forza* applied to them. (Cf. *Discourses*, p. 271.) *Forza* applied to a lever, reminding us of the worker's physical effort, evokes the etymology of the word (deriving from the Latin *fortis*), and Galileo frequently uses it where physical strength is implied. Thus he refers to the *forza* of a draft animal turning a capstan (one of his simple machines) and even, simply, to the *forza* of a horse; in drawing wire, workers pull it through the draw-plate with great *forza;* a thread held between the fingers does not slip even when pulled with considerable *forza*. (*Mechanics*, pp. 150, 161; *Discourses*, pp. 9, 53.) By an extension of meaning analogous to that in English, he can speak of the *forza* of a discourse and the *forza* of truth. (*Ibid.*, pp. 165, 164.) On occasion *forza* can take on an inanimate, almost generalized usage. In the *Dialogue* Tycho's conundrum of the cannon is solved by a thought experiment with crossbows in a moving carriage; Galileo argues that if the strength (not *forza* here) of the bow is the same for shots forward and backward, the arrows will fall equal distances from the carriage. So also with cannon shots to east and west on a turning earth when they are made with the same *forza*. (*Dialogue*, p. 171.) Without a pause he moves from the strength of the bow to the *forza* of the cannon.

Interested as he was in the mathematics of simple machines, Galileo found it convenient to substitute weights for animate *forze,* and he finds no difficulty in referring to the *forza* of a weight, or in employing the words "weight" and "*forza*" interchangeably. (Cf. *Discourses*, p. 10; *Opere*, VIII, 339.) On at least one occasion, however, *forze* refers to the mechanical advantages of levers. (*Discourses*, p. 124. Cf. *Dialogue*, pp. 214–215.) It would not, then, be far from the truth to say that Galileo has a clear conception of static force, if not a wholly consistent use of the word *forza* to express it. If "resistance" is usually applied to the other end, the two ends of a lever are indistinguishable to mathematical analysis, and his discussion of the resistance or breaking strength of beams can refer to the *forza* of a vacuum. (*Discourses*, p. 15.)

A body in motion can also manifest *forza*, as Galileo's investigation of the *forza* of percussion suggests. In the *Dialogue*, Simplicio declares that a man throwing a stone moves his arm with speed and *forza* so that the resulting impetus carries the stone along, and Sagredo asks why a hoop thrown with a cord goes farther and consequently with more *forza* than one thrown by hand. (*Dialogue*, pp. 151, 158.) The suggestion that, somehow, the *forza* of the projector is conserved in the projectile, is clearly stated in fragments accompanying the so-called sixth day of the *Discourses*. Thus large bells can be put in motion only by repeated pulls, each of which adds *forza* to that acquired from earlier pulls; the larger the bell, the more *forza* it acquires. A smaller bell, more easily set in motion, also comes to rest more quickly, not being saturated, so to speak, by so much *forza* as the larger one. (*Opere*, VIII, 346. Cf. also p. 345.) The lever provides the bridge from statics to dynamics, and supplies a measure of the *forza* of motion. Galileo's analysis of it in terms of virtual velocities suggests the term mv (if I may employ the anachronism—Galileo does not, of course, clearly define mass). His word *momento* serves both for our "moment" and for our "momentum," and he frequently uses *impeto* for "momentum." One of his standard devices to measure the *momenti* of equal bodies is to compare the impacts they make—that is their *forze* of percussion. In the *Discourses*, moreover, the investigation of the instantaneous velocities of projectiles at various points in their trajectories leads Sagredo to declare that now he can calculate the *forze* necessary to fire projectiles over given ranges; in the context he can only mean that the *forza* is equal to the momentum that must be generated in the projectile. (*Discourses*, p. 286. Cf. pp. 273–275.) If we had only this declaration, we should have to say that Galileo equates force to Δmv. Certainly this is the earliest suggestion of that equation, precisely Newton's statement of the second law, of which I know. The converse is stated in Viviani's interpolated passage—that the *impeto* or *momento* of a body is equal to the *forza* just sufficient to stop it. (*Ibid.*, p. 183.) So also in a discussion of inclined planes he states that the *impeto* acquired by a body at the bottom of such a plane is equal to that necessary to drive the body back to the same height; hence we may conclude that as much *forza* is necessary to raise the body through the same vertical height by any path. (*Opere*, VIII, 338.) It is worth noting that while Galileo sometimes refers to instantaneous *forza*, he is more prone to use the word in the context above, with a dimension of time built in, what I will call "total force." Thus *forza* in the last three examples is equal most profligate in their multiplicity, serve equally well when the spirit moves. When asked by Galileo to expand a passage in the *Discourses*, Viviani finds himself embarrassed by the verbal wealth; and whether from sheer exuberance at the extent of his choice or from despair at its imprecision he refers to "l'impeto, il talento, l'energia," or we might say "il momento" of a moving body.[6] What does he mean when he uses the words *we might say?* Better, we have said already—we have said more than once—we have said as well "la virtù," "la velocità," "la propensione al moto." I repeat, however, that the question is not one of terminology. Galileo is creating a new physics; its terminology is not ready at hand. He must create it as well, and it hardly behooves us to judge the process by those in-

to the total change of momentum ($\triangle$mv), not to its rate of change. I must add, however, that Galileo also states in the *Discourses* that the velocity of a moving body, even if its *forza* is small, can overcome the great resistance of a slowly moving body if the ratio of the velocities is greater than the ratio of the resistance to the *forza*—a return to *forza* as static weight. (*Discourses*, p. 291.)

One other use of *forza* requires comment. Galileo continues to think in medieval terms of forced or violent motion as the opposite of natural motion. Thus a ball spontaneously moves down a slope and *forza* is necessary to keep it at rest; if it is to move up the slope, more *forza* is needed. (Cf. *Dialogue*, pp. 147, 264.) The *forza* that holds a body outside its natural place, he says in the youthful *De motu*, must be equal to its weight. (*De motu*, p. 98.) This of course repeats the conditions of equilibrium in the balance and suggests further the use of *forza* as that which overcomes "resistance" with the lever. When a rope is "violated" by enough *forza*, it breaks. (*Discourses*, pp. 121–122.) A similar use of *forza* apppears in discussions of projectile motion. Birds in flight are treated as a special instance of such motion; Salviati declares that the use of birds in flight as an argument against the rotation of the earth depends on their being animate and able to use *forza* at will against the original inherent motion of terrestrial objects. (*Dialogue*, p. 186.) Similarly he argues that the motion of a ship is not identical to the rotation of the earth; while the latter motion is natural, the motion of the ship is accidental, conferred as it is by the *forza* of the oars. (*Dialogue*, p. 142.)

[6] *Discourses*, p. 181.

sights gleaned from our freshman course in physics. The question of interest is whether we can find a concept of force behind the confusion of terms. Does Galileo arrive at a generalization similar to or approaching Newton's second law, such that for every change of motion, however much the circumstances may differ, we can say that an external force has been exerted on a body? To employ my figure one last time, this is the familiar creature the visitor from the latter years of the century expects to find. In its place he discovers instead a strange breed of monsters roaming the countryside, also called by a wide assortment of names but perhaps most frequently by "a natural tendency" (*naturale inclinazione*) to motion.

My questions then are two in number. To what extent does Galileo approach the concept of force despite his strange and unexpected terms? And why does he not succeed in formulating it more fully? At first blush they appear to be thoroughly outrageous questions for a historian to ask—somewhat akin to asking why the Thirty Years War did not last forty years, or what would have been the fate of Ptolemaic Egypt had Cleopatra been flat-chested. The historian examines the past that was; he leaves speculation about the past that might have been to Monday morning quarterbacks with nothing better to occupy their time. I submit, however, that the concept of force did come to exist and in a philosophic framework similar in many ways to that held by Galileo. Answers to my questions should help us better to understand the exact nature of his accomplishment. And if I may be allowed to repeat once more that I am a Newtonian scholar on vacation, the answers to my questions should also help me to comprehend the exact nature of what the rest of the century accomplished.

Let us look closely at Galileo's "natural tendencies" to motion. There are two of them, and it is not too much to say that they constitute the heart and soul of his physics. On close examination the two tendencies reveal themselves as radically different things. Although Galileo refers on occasion to the "natural tendency" of terrestrial objects to circle the earth's center once a day, he prefers other language. "Keeping up with the earth," he declares in the *Dialogue*, "is the primordial and eternal motion ineradicably and inseparably participated in by this ball as a terrestrial object, which it has by its nature and will possess forever." [7] Analyses of other horizontal motions make use of similar terms. A stone carried by a ship, for example, has "an ineradicable motion" as fast as that of the ship.[8] Horizontal motion, however natural, cannot generate itself; it can only persevere. If there are difficulties in Galileo's treatment of it, as I shall want to discuss later, we can safely neglect Galileo's language and translate his "natural and eternal" horizontal motion as inertial motion, granting always that to Galileo inertial motion is circular motion around a gravitational center.

We cannot so easily dispose of the other "natural tendency," nor shall we wish to if we hope to find anything resembling a concept of force. Whatever the various phrases by which he refers to it,[9] the "natural tendency" of

[7] *Dialogue*, pp. 177–178.

[8] *Ibid.*, p. 148.

[9] The parts of the earth do not move toward the center of the universe "but so as to unite with the whole earth (and . . . consequently they have a natural tendency [*naturale inclinazione*] toward the center of the terrestrial globe, by which tendency they cooperate to form and preserve it). . . ." Thus the earth is a sphere. Why not believe that the sun and moon, *et al.*, are also round because of a "concordant instinct [*concorde instinto*] and natural tendency [*concorso naturale*] of all their component parts?" If a part is removed and separated, is it not reasonable to believe that it would "return spontaneously and by natural tendency [*naturale instinto*]?" (*Ibid.*, pp. 33–34.) He suggests further that the parts of the earth "move to their whole, their universal mother." (*Ibid.*, p. 37.)

heavy bodies to move toward a center of gravity reminds us of the animism of premechanical conceptions of nature, the very antithesis of the concept of an external force which determines the motion of inert matter. If we ignore the animism for the moment, however, and examine his analysis of free fall, we find that weight functions in it as what we now call force. I do not refer merely to the fact known by all that Galileo defines the uniformly accelerated motion of a falling body. I mean far more the conclusion that will always be associated with the Tower of Pisa, whether or not Galileo ever conducted experiments from it—that in a vacuum all heavy bodies fall with the same uniform acceleration. The first conclusion does not necessitate the second. More than the first, it is the second that makes Galileo's analysis of weight in free fall the prototype of the later concept of force.

A comparison of Galileo's final position with his early *De motu* reveals how great is the step he has taken. *De motu* repeats the proposition of Aristotelian mechanics, that velocity of fall is proportional to weight. It is true, of course, that, following Benedetti, he means "specific gravity" when he says "weight," and indeed the specific gravity of the falling body minus that of the medium. Nevertheless, he explicitly sets velocity proportional to weight, and in expounding the proposition he displays in its clearest form the essentially static nature of this dynamics. If a body is projected upward, it can only be that lightness has been impressed upon it, lightness that temporarily preponderates over its heaviness. If it is held in midair, the impressed lightness must equal the heaviness of the body. During acceleration, which is held to be temporary and limited to the initial moments of fall, the decay of impressed lightness is paralleled by the increase in velocity. Galileo later puts a point of view not wholly dissimilar into the mouth of Simplicio when the latter is made to assert that a body added to another causes the combined body to fall faster. Not only is velocity the direct transposition of static weight from the point of view of this dynamics, but static weight continues to function as static weight even during fall. At the same time it moves the body and continues to bear down as weight. Galileo wants to have his weight and eat it, too, so to speak. The characteristics of a dynamic situation are not really distinguished from those of a static one. If we forget for a moment what we know about Galileo's ultimate conclusions and try to imagine how the author of *De motu* would be most likely to define uniformly accelerated motion, we can, I believe, see no reason why the earlier point of view cannot be extended to the new conception of motion. If he can hold velocities to be proportional to weights, so he can hold accelerations proportional to weights. Such a position is by no means impossible; Salviati temporarily assumes it for polemic purposes in the *Dialogue,* and Galileo has Sagredo accept it there as obvious until Salviati disabuses him.[10] That Galileo does not adopt it is owing to his recognition of the difference between the static and the dynamic effects of the force of weight.

As Salviati says to Simplicio,

> . . . it is necessary to distinguish between heavy bodies in motion and the same bodies at rest. A large stone placed in a balance not only acquires additional weight by having another stone placed upon it, but even by the addition of a handful of hemp its weight is augmented six to ten ounces according to the quantity of hemp. But if you tie the hemp to the stone and allow them to fall freely from some height, do you believe that the hemp will press down upon the stone and thus accelerate its motion or do you think the motion will be retarded by a partial upward pressure? One always feels the pressure upon his shoulders when he prevents the motion of a load resting upon him; but if one

[10] *Ibid.*, p. 202.

descends just as rapidly as the load would fall how can it gravitate or press upon him? Do you not see that this would be the same as trying to strike a man with a lance when he is running away from you with a speed which is equal to, or even greater, than that with which you are following him? [11]

Galileo's analysis contains two elements of interest. In the first place, since the time of *De motu* he has formed a rudimentary distinction between weight and mass. Salviati's expositions to Simplicio suggest how atomism may have helped him to arrive at it. Every body can be imagined as a collection, more or less large, of atoms, each of which has a natural tendency as a heavy body to move toward the center of the earth with the common acceleration.[12] The weight of a body can only be increased by adding more atoms and thus increasing at the same rate the quantity of matter to be moved by the weight.[13] The equal

[11] *Discourses,* pp. 63–64. Cf. a passage from the sixth day: in an attempt to measure the force of percussion he sets up a large balance, on one side of which two buckets are hung, one below the other. Initially the top bucket is full of water, which runs out through a hole in the bottom and falls into the lower one. The water that is in the air does not affect the balance, Galileo says, "because, with the motion of the falling water continually accelerating, the higher parts are not able to gravitate and press on the lower ones. . . ." (*Opere,* VIII, 325.)

[12] Cf. also a passage in *Mechanics,* in which he defines heaviness (*gravità*) as the tendency to move naturally downward which, in solid bodies, is caused by the greater or lesser abundance of matter of which they are constituted. (*Mechanics,* p. 151.)

[13] Cf. his discussion of the frequency of vibrations of strings. For a given length and tension, if we wish to make one string sound an octave lower than another string made of the same material, we must make the first string four times as large. If we change the material, however, we must make the first string four times as heavy. Thus a brass string an octave lower than a gut string may have a smaller diameter. If two spinets are strung, one with gold wire and the other with brass, and if the corresponding strings are all of the same length, diameter, and tension, the spinet strung with gold will have a pitch

acceleration of all bodies merely expresses the constant ratio of weight to quantity of matter. Like Newton later in the century, Galileo realizes that in the pendulum he has an instrument to measure the constancy of the ratio with great accuracy.

The second and more explicit point in the analysis is Galileo's identification of the dynamic action of the force of weight in exactly the terms we continue to use. The total action of the force of weight manifests itself in the motion it produces; none of it is left over to act as weight in pressing on a body falling with it. In an early version of *De motu* the greater velocity of the heavier body is justified on the principle that the greater cause produces a greater effect.[14] Galileo now recognizes that the greater effect appears not in the velocity, but in the quantity of motion— in our terms, in the momentum.[15] Such a conclusion is not

about a fifth lower because the density of gold is about twice that of brass. "And here it is to be noted that it is the weight rather than the size of a moving body which offers resistance to change of motion [*velocità del moto*—the word change does not appear in the Italian]." (*Discourses*, pp. 102–103.)

[14] *De motu*, p. 31.

[15] It is fascinating to watch Galileo struggle to keep his insight clear in his own mind, and the spectacle instructs us anew to appreciate the immense difficulty it presents to him as well as to others. When he expounds the effect of media on the motion of falling bodies in the *Discourses*, he slips back into at least the terminology of *De motu*. After explaining to Simplicio in no uncertain terms that velocities of falling bodies are not in constant ratio to specific gravities because velocities continually increase, he forgets it all three pages later as he examines the fall of bodies differing in density through dense media. Ebony is a thousand times as heavy as air whereas an inflated bladder is only four times as heavy. Therefore air diminishes "the inherent and natural speed [*sic!*]" (*intrinseca e naturale velocità*) of ebony by one-thousandth, and diminishes that of the bladder by one-fourth. When a piece of ebony reaches the ground from a tower of two hundred cubits, the bladder will have fallen only three-quarters of the distance. Lead is twelve times as heavy as water, ivory twice as heavy. The "speeds" (*assoluto velocità*) of the two, equal when they fall unhindered, are diminished when they fall in water, that of lead by one-twelfth,

necessarily implied in the concept of uniformly accelerated motion. An independent insight, it establishes the proto-type of the later general concept of force.

The analysis of the dynamics of fall is never far from Galileo's mind. The frequent assertion that his physics is basically a kinematics appears mistaken to me. At all its critical points it returns explicitly to its foundation in dynamics. At the very beginning, when Salviati defines uniformly accelerated motion, he assures Sagredo that it is not an arbitrary motion such as a mathematician might define but a motion that actually occurs in nature. The other basic motion, uniform motion, is on a horizontal plane in which, as he frequently repeats, there is neither a tendency to motion nor a repugnance to it—that is, mo-tion in which the force of weight does not operate to pro-duce any change. When Galileo comes to the proposition, crucial for his entire physics, that the gain or loss of motion depends only on vertical displacement to or from the center of the earth, regardless of the path followed, he once again abandons kinematics for dynamics, as Professor Dijkster-huis has shown. Far from limiting himself to kinematics, it appears to me that Galileo attempts—with almost infinite ingenuity, I must add—to extend his analysis of the dy-namics of fall throughout physics and to make it the stand-ard by which other motions can be measured.

that of ivory by one-half. While lead falls through eleven cubits of water, ivory will fall through only six. (*Discourses*, p. 76.) It is necessary for me to comment, however, that if we replace "speed" by "instantaneous velocity" at a given time, all the figures are correct. Indeed, Galileo's mathematics, which works with geometric ratios, almost forces him into comparisons of this sort. In this instance time is taken as the constant and the unit of time in each instance is that necessary for the denser body to complete its fall. When the times of fall for the two bodies are equal, both the velocity and the space traversed by the less dense body will be to those of the more dense in the same ratio as the relative specific gravities—i.e., as the effective forces.

He extends it, for example, to other accelerations. Free fall, of course, offers no variation in acceleration. The constant proportion of weight to the quantity of matter moved gives all bodies the same acceleration in free fall. That is, it gives them the same acceleration when they fall through a vacuum. Vacuums are never available, however; real bodies fall in media, and media check their rate of acceleration. In correcting Aristotle's exposition of a medium's retarding effect, Galileo relies on his analysis of the dynamics of free fall. It is perhaps the first intellectual dividend that he reaps from it. Extending the Archimedean approach of *De motu* into his new conception of motion, he treats the effect of a medium as a decrease in the effective force of weight. Not the absolute weight of a body but its relative weight in the medium is what moves it down. Without even pausing to justify the step, he sets the acceleration proportional to the effective force of weight. So also in the analysis of inclined planes. Having derived the component of the force of weight that acts parallel to the plane, he sets the acceleration down the plane proportional to it.[16] The case of the inclined plane is of great im-

[16] The *impeto* acting on a body in descent, Salviati asserts, is equal to the resistance or least force sufficient to hold it at rest. To measure the force and resistance he uses the weight of another body, H, which descends vertically while the body G moves up the plane. Because they are connected by a cord over a pulley, both must move equal distances. G does not move an equal vertical distance, however, and it exerts its resistance only along the vertical. It has no resistance along the horizontal because motion in that plane involves no change in its distance from the center of the earth. In a state of equilibrium, therefore, the *momenti*, the *velocità*, and the *propensioni al moto* must be in inverse ratio to the weights. As he says, this is demonstrable in every instance of mechanical motion. When the weights are in this ratio, they will have *momenti eguali*. Since it is agreed that *l'impeto, l'energia, il momento, o la propensione al moto* of a moving body is equal to the force or resistance sufficient to stop it, and since the *momento totale* of H is along the perpendicular, H is the exact measure of the *momento parziale* which G exerts along the plane. But the measure of the *total*

portance to Galileo. Inclined planes are more readily manipulated than media. The degree of incline is capable of infinite variation between the vertical and the horizontal, and Galileo has at his disposal a measure for every acceleration from zero to g. There is more than a small suggestion that he considers accelerations above g preternatural and beyond analysis. The formula with which we are all familiar, that acceleration is proportional to force, cannot emerge directly from the ideal case of free fall in which acceleration is always constant. If it can be derived indirectly from such an instance, it appears directly only in those where media or inclined planes vary the force of weight without altering the quantity of matter.

When Galileo discusses parabolic trajectories, he applies the dynamics of fall to the measurement of horizontal motion. In any given trajectory one specific horizontal motion compounds with the uniformly accelerated motion of a freely falling body. If we adopt the vertex of the parabola as our origin, the latter motion, starting from rest, is

momento of G is its weight, and therefore the ratio of the *impeto o momento parziale* of G to its *impeto massimo e totale* is the ratio of H to G (which equals the sine of the angle of inclination). (*Ibid.*, pp. 182–183.) The passage is actually written by Viviani, at the suggestion of Galileo. Its content is repeated exactly in a later demonstration that appears in Galileo's original Latin. After demonstrating from kinematics that bodies will fall in equal times along all chords of a circle drawn to its lowest point, he adds that the same conclusion can also be demonstrated from "mechanics" (*ex mechanicis*). From the lowest point, A, of the vertical diameter of a circle, two chords are drawn such that AC is longer than AD. AB, equal to AD, is laid off on AC. "From the principles of mechanics" (*ex elementis mechanicis*) the *momentum ponderis* along ABC is to *momentum suum totale* as BE/BA. And along AD the same ratio is DF/DA or DF/BA. The ratios on both chords represent the vertical rise of the chords to their total length. Therefore *eiusdem ponderis momentum* along ABC is to its *momentum* along AD as BE/DF. Therefore the distances traversed in equal times along ABC and AD are as BE/DF. But it can be shown that AC/AD is equal to BE/DF. Therefore the times of descent along all chords are equal. (*Ibid.*, pp. 189–190.)

wholly defined; but the nature of the individual parabola
will depend on the one unchanging horizontal velocity
with which the acceleration compounds. How can that
velocity be specified without ambiguity? There is nothing
simpler from our point of view—we have only to state our
units and to measure the velocity in feet or meters or what-
have-you per second. To Galileo, who works within a geometric rather than an algebraic framework, and who deals
with ratios rather than numbers, such a solution simply
does not present itself. He arrives instead at the concept of
sublimity. Because the acceleration of falling bodies is constant, "the speed of a body falling from the same elevation
is always one and the same," [17] and the horizontal velocity

[17] *Ibid.*, p. 260. Cf. also p. 264: "Concerning motions and their
velocities or momenta (*impeti*) whether uniform or naturally accelerated, one cannot speak definitely until he has established a measure
for such velocities and also for time. As for time we have the already
widely adopted hours, first minutes and second minutes. So for
velocities, just as for intervals of time, there is need of a common
standard which shall be understood and accepted by everyone, and
which shall be the same for all. As has already been stated, the Author
considers the velocity of a freely falling body adapted to this purpose,
since this velocity increases according to the same law in all parts
of the world; thus for instance the speed acquired by a leaden ball of a
pound weight starting from rest and falling vertically through the
height of, say, a spear's length is the same in all places; it is therefore
excellently adapted for representing the momentum [*impeto*] acquired
in the case of natural fall." It is relevant to my argument to note
that the discussion, which starts as a discussion of velocity and employs
such terms as *impeto o grado di velocità* and *velocità ed impeto* (p. 266)
subtly changes its tone. If the *impeto* of a body moving vertically is
three units it "would . . . strike [*arebbe percossa*] the horizontal plane
with a *forza* of three. If it has in addition a horizontal component of
five it would strike [*il colpo sarà come quello del percuziente moto*]
with a *velocità e forza* of five. At any point on a parabola except the
vertex the *impeto e percossa* exceeds both the vertical and horizontal
percossa dell'impeto. (Pp. 267–268.) The discussion continues for
several pages, now wholly concerned with the percussive force that
accompanies velocity. A kinematic discussion has transformed itself into
a dynamic discussion.

of a body can be stated in terms of its sublimity, the distance through which it must fall to acquire that velocity. Through the concept of sublimity the dynamics of fall furnishes a standard of horizontal velocity.

How little Galileo thinks of free fall in purely kinematic terms is evident whenever he wishes to measure velocity. When he is demonstrating to Simplicio that a body falling does not instantaneously acquire a finite velocity, he proposes a thought experiment on its power to drive a stake into the ground; and again when he wants to determine whether the terminal velocity of a body falling in air is less than the muzzle velocity of a cannonball, he calls upon their percussive effects. Similarly the determination of momenta at different points in a parabolic trajectory transforms itself unconsciously, it appears, into a discussion of what Galileo calls the force of percussion.[18] The measurements are to be rough and ready in these instances —how far the stake is driven, how much the cannonball is flattened. Galileo is interested as well in the precise measurement of the force of percussion, and as he examines the problem its ambiguities strike him. Can we say that two blows against differing resistances are equal when the one drives a nail two inches and the other only one inch? No, we cannot, since the differing velocities of the receding nails alter the force with which the blow strikes. Can we then establish standards of percussion and resistance by which we can analyze percussive force? Fortunately we can, and once again the dynamics of fall supplies the need. The force of a heavy body falling from a given height is always the same. So also is the resistance of a heavy body to being raised.[19] The equipment Galileo devises, and which he analyzes without apparently conducting actual experiments, consists of a pulley and two heavy bodies. The heav-

[18] See note 17.
[19] *Opere*, VIII, 338.

ier body rests on a table and a cord from it passes over the pulley to the lighter body. When the second body is dropped, the force of its percussion in snapping the cord is transmitted over the pulley and operates to raise the first body. Galileo's analysis repeats the same process for simple machines. The velocity of the smaller body can compensate for its deficiency in weight. If the ratio of velocities exceeds the ratio of weights, it will be able to move the resistance at least some small distance. But the ratio of velocities cannot fail to be greater since the larger body is at rest (an ambiguity at least as involved as that of the stake, but one which he chooses to ignore).[20] Thus a small body, say of ten pounds, is able to drive a resistance equal to that which a hundred-pound body has to being lifted, but the distance it drives the resistance will be one-tenth of the distance it falls. If the resistance is equal to two hundred pounds, the body of ten pounds will drive it one-twentieth of the distance it falls.[21] He concludes then that the force of percussion is potentially infinite since any body, no matter how small, should be able to move any resistance it strikes, no matter how large the resistance is.

Galileo's solution of percussion employs the quantity that emerges from the investigation of simple machines—the product of the size of the body and its velocity.[22] We

[20] *Ibid.*, VIII, 332–333.

[21] *Ibid.*, VIII, 341.

[22] Not only in his *Mechanics* but in the *Discourses* and elsewhere Galileo reveals how important the lever is for seventeenth-century efforts to reduce motion to quantitative treatment. The law of the lever (with its special case, the balance) is the one apparently certain rule of mechanics with which the century starts. By means of the principle of virtual velocities, Galileo extends it to all the simple machines, even to the problems of hydrostatics. In all instances, the governing principle is the equality of the product mv at one end of the lever to that at the other. The *momento* (moment) of the lever thus easily transforms itself into the *momento* (momentum) of the moving body. A possibility of serious ambiguity is built into the lever, and Galileo, together with the whole century following him, slips into it unaware. Since

both ends of the lever move in identical time without acceleration, it is immaterial whether one uses the virtual velocities of the two weights or forces or their virtual displacements. Velocities must be in the same proportion as displacements. Although Galileo often uses displacement, it is clear that he means it as a substitute for velocity; and whenever he states the general principle of the lever, he states it in terms of velocity. It is all too easy, however, to forget that the equivalence holds only for the lever and analogous instances in which a mechanical connection insures that each body moves for the same time, and in which, because of equilibrium, the motion involved is virtual motion, not accelerated motion. In the so-called sixth day of the *Discourses*, Galileo, who remarks so forcibly the intimate connection of motion and time, forgets—and his whole analysis of percussion is correspondingly vitiated. Galileo begins by restating the law of the inclined plane which he has derived from the lever. A body of ten pounds descending vertically can balance one of one hundred pounds on an inclined plane the length of which is ten times its elevation. Therefore, he continues, "drop a body of ten pounds through any vertical distance; the impetus it acquires, when applied to a body of one hundred pounds, will drive it an equal distance up the inclined plane that involves a vertical rise equal to one-tenth its length. It was concluded above that a force able to drive a body up an inclined plane is sufficient to drive it vertically a distance equal to the elevation of the inclined plane, in this case a tenth part of the distance traversed on the incline, which distance on the incline is equal to the fall of the first body of ten pounds. Thus it is manifest that the vertical fall of a body of ten pounds is sufficient to raise a body of one hundred pounds vertically, but only through a space equal to one tenth of its descent." (*Opere*, VIII, 340–341.) His statement of the force of percussion, cited in the text, repeats this conclusion. The case of free fall is not, of course, identical to the conditions of equilibrium on the plane because the times involved are not identical and because two separate, accelerated motions take place. If there is an equality of the products of weight $\times$ distance (that is, in our terms, work), there cannot be an equality of momenta (mv) but rather of kinetic energies ($\frac{1}{2} mv^2$). From the ambiguity of the lever springs the argument between quantity of motion and *vis viva* in which the second half of the century engages.

It is interesting to see Galileo attempt to probe the ambiguity in fragments that seem to postdate his essay on the force of percussion. In every mobile there are two types of resistance—the first deriving from the internal resistance by which one thousand pounds is lifted with more difficulty than is one hundred pounds, the second deriving from the distance through which it must be moved (so that more force is required to hurl a stone one hundred feet than fifty feet). To the two resistances correspond two different motors—one moves by commit an anachronism, of course, in referring to it as "momentum," since Galileo has only a dim perception of mass. Nevertheless, it is an anachronism which greatly facilitates our expression without seriously violating his thought. Both the words *impeto* and *momento* do service in expressing the concept. Galileo's use of "momentum" is ambiguous. If the consequences of the principle of inertia are rigorously drawn, the momentum of a body can be nothing more than a conventional term that expresses the force (to us, though not to Galileo, the integral of Fdt) required to generate or to destroy the body's motion. Galileo's use of "momentum" can often be interpreted in this way. The temptation constantly presents itself, however, to think of it as a force transferred from the original mover and internalized in the body, a force that keeps it moving. Thus the bob of a pendulum "propelled by its own *impeto*" passes the perpendicular and mounts to its original height.[23] One cannot fail to sense how profoundly the medieval concept of impetus expresses our perception of motion. Galileo is unable wholly to liberate himself from it, and even half a century later Newton defines inertia as *vis insita*. Momentum can be imparted to a body by any mover, by a cannon, for example, or by a human hand. As the pendulum, the inclined plane, and many other examples illustrate,

pressing without striking, while the other strikes. The first moves a limited resistance but through infinite space, following it always with the same force. The second moves any resistance but through a limited distance. Hence the distance rather than the resistance is proportional to the percussive body, whereas the resistance rather than the distance is proportional to the pressure. Galileo concludes by denying the whole of his essay on percussion and doubting that any proportion, by which they can measure each other, exists between the two motors or forces. (*Opere*, VIII, 343.) In his pressure we can see the balance and in his infinite steady motion the condition of equilibrium from which derives the quantity mv. In his percussive force proportional to distance we can see the product, Fs. which we call work.

[23] *Dialogue*, p. 151.

it can also be generated in a falling body by the force of weight. Certainly it can be given precise expression in the case of free fall, and again the force of weight offers itself as a standard for other forces.[24]

[24] The verbs that Galileo uses with "momentum" reveal the active sense he often gives it. The *impeto* that the bob of a pendulum acquires in descending with a natural motion is able "to drive it upward by a forced motion" (*sospignere di moto violento*) through an equal ascent. (*Ibid.*, p. 227.) In general, when a heavy body falls from any height, it acquires just as much *impeto* as was necessary "to carry it" (*tirarlo*) to that height. (*Discourses*, p. 94.) When a ball is thrown, the *moto* (a few lines later the *impeto*) is conserved in it and continues "to urge it" (*condurlo*) on. (*Dialogue*, p. 156.) A point on the circumference of a moving wheel has the *impeto* with which "to hurl" (*scagliare*) a stone. (*Ibid.*, p. 213.) Water in a barge, set in oscillation by an unequal motion, rises at one end, is forced by its weight to fall again, but, "pushed" (*promossa*) by its own *impeto* goes beyond equilibrium. (*Ibid.*, p. 428.) In discussing the hypothetical case of a ball rotating around the earth once a day, he even refers to the *virtù* that makes it go around. (*Ibid.*, p. 233.) See also the example quoted in note 19, in which he imagines the *impeto* acquired by one body in falling to be transferred to another of different weight and "to drive" (*cacciare*) that one upward.

One can follow the derivation of "momentum" from the moment of a weight or force on a lever. He states the principle of simple machines in his *Mechanics:* "that whatever is gained in force by their means is lost in time and speed." (*Mechanics*, p. 176.) In the same work he justifies the concept of virtual velocities by saying, "It is not foreign to the arrangement of nature that the speed of the motion of the heavy body B should compensate the greater resistance of the weight A when this moves more weakly to D and the other descends more rapidly to E. . . . And from this reasoning we may arrive at the knowledge that the speed of motion is capable of increasing *momento* in the movable body in the same proportion as that in which this speed of motion is increased." (*Ibid.*, p. 156.) In his *Discourse on Bodies in Water* he defines *momento* in a way that includes both moment and momentum—"*Momento*, among mechanics, signifies that *virtù*, that *forza*, that *efficacia*, with which the mover moves and the moved body resists. Which *virtù* depends not only upon simple heaviness, but upon the speed of motion, and upon the varying inclinations of the space over which the motion is made, as a descending body has more *impeto* in a very steep descent than in one less steep." (Galileo, *Discourse on Bodies in Water*, trans. by Thomas Salusbury, ed. by Stillman Drake

We are now in a position to answer the first of the two questions I asked—to what extent does Galileo approach

[Urbana, 1960], p. 6; I quote a modern translation by Stillman Drake in his introduction to *Mechanics*, p. 145, but the original Italian words are my insertions.) In the same work he applies virtual velocities to hydrostatics and demonstrates that in a confined vessel a body can float in a quantity of water that weighs less than the body. The proposition may appear to be a paradox. "But he that shall but comprehend of what Importance Velocity of Motion is, and how it exactly compensates the defect and want of Gravity, will cease to wonder. . . ." (*Bodies in Water*, p. 16.) In the *Dialogue* the concept finally frees itself entirely from its connection with the balance and lever. Starting with the balance and lever, Galileo states that "the *momento* and the *forza* of a moving body of say four pounds are as much as those of a body weighing one hundred, whenever the former has one hundred units of speed and the latter only four units." He proceeds to a general statement "that the resistance coming from the speed of motion compensates that which depends upon the weight of another moving body, and consequently that a body weighing one pound and moving with a speed of one hundred units resists restraint (*resiste all'esser frenato*) as much as another of one hundred pounds whose speed is but a single unit. And two equal movable bodies will equally resist being moved if they are to be made to move with equal speed. But if one is to move faster than the other, it will make the greater resistance according as the greater speed is to be conferred upon it." The analysis is immediately separated from the lever and applied to centrifugal force. When two unequal wheels turn so that the rims move with equal linear velocities, the smaller wheel ought to be more powerful to project a stone on it; "to deviate a moving body from a motion for which it has the *impeto*, is not a greater or a lesser *forza* needed, according as the deviation must be greater or less? That is, according as they must in this deviation pass through a greater or a lesser space in a given time?" To which rhetorical question by Salviati, Sagredo replies, "Yes, for it was already concluded above that in order to make a body move, the faster it is to be moved the greater must be the moving force (*virtù movente*)." (*Dialogue*, pp. 214–216.) One cannot avoid recognizing here an implicit equation between momentum and the action or force that can generate or destroy it; with centrifugal force, momentum is conceived vectorially, which is of course wholly atypical with Galileo. It is worth remarking again that force in this context does not mean an instantaneous force, which generates an acceleration, but what I will call a total force (the integral of Fdt in our terms), which generates a finite momentum.

the concept of force? His analysis of the dynamics of fall, despite the rubrics in which it appears, furnishes the proto-type for the later concept of force. He attempts to use the dynamics of fall as a standard to measure other mo-tions. On occasion he implies the similarity of free fall to other accelerated motions, for example, the acceleration of a galley under the repeated strokes of the oars, or the in-creasing motion of a bell under repeated pulls of the rope. Nevertheless, he never formulates a general concept of force such that every accelerated motion shares in common the condition that force is being exercised. This he does not do; this he cannot do. He cannot do it because motion toward a gravitating center remains for him a metaphys-ically privileged motion to which the adjective "natural" testifies on virtually every page that he writes. Galileo does not equate the acceleration of fall with other instances in which motions are generated; he only uses it as a standard by which to measure them. It is surely significant that he never tries to analyze other motions in similar terms. When he discusses projectiles, he imagines the horizontal compo-nent to derive from some fall. One might look for some time to find such a projectile. The known projectiles in this world are almost all set in motion by other agencies—a throwing arm, a bow string, gun powder. Galileo knows this, of course, but he never suggests that such sources be subjected to the same analysis as fall. He merely accepts the resultant motion and measures it by a sublimity. He does not, I repeat, formulate a general concept of force.

The lack of it is nowhere more evident than in his treatment of friction. Galileo's description of the action of a medium on a projectile moving through it reminds us of the force of weight acting on a body as it ascends an inclined plane. The friction or resistance of the medium destroys part of the projectile's motion. Friction, that is to say, is a force. To *us* it is a force, but Galileo does not suggest that it has anything in common with the "natural tendency" of a body to descend. He treats it instead as an obstruction that adulterates and obscures the pure mathematical relations of motion. Of the accidents from which resistance derives, infinite in number, he says, "it is not possible to give any exact description; hence, in order to handle this matter in a scientific way, it is necessary to cut loose from these difficulties; and having discovered and demonstrated the theorems in the case of no resistance, to use them and apply them with such limitations as experience will teach." [25] Far from being a force, friction, to Galileo, is only an unpleasant nuisance.

The answer to the second question must necessarily be more speculative. Why does Galileo not succeed in formulating more fully a concept of force? I believe that three factors operate to inhibit him. The first is mathematical. When we think of force, we think of the formulae $F = ma$ or $F = \dfrac{d}{dt} mv$, and we think of the operations of algebra and of calculus by which we can calculate its quantity. It is hard to imagine the limitations that Galileo's geometrical method imposes upon him. With one exception his diagrams show the path of the moving body. Since time and velocity change uniformly, he can set them proportional to lines and easily formulate ratios to compare them. He is fortunate to have only one ratio in which a squared quantity appears, the increase of distance in relation to time, and the simple device of the mean proportional renders it amenable to treatment. There is nowhere for the quantities of acceleration and force to appear. The one exception to his usual diagram is the familiar triangular representa-

[25] *Discourses*, pp. 252–253. Cf. his discussion of the resistance of the ground to a stake driven into it: it always increases as the stake penetrates "and in a proportion wholly unknown (*ignotissima*) due to the divers accidents that arise from the varying degrees of hardness . . . in the earth. . . ." (*Opere*, VIII, 338.)

tion of time and velocity, in which the area of the triangle represents distance, and here again nothing in the diagram corresponds to force or acceleration. Half a century later Newton has to transcend a similar geometric representation in a large number of problems, and to represent force by a new curve, which he can integrate, constructed along one axis and having nothing in common with the rest of the diagram except the paper on which it is drawn. Galileo does not have this option open to him. Small wonder that he limits himself to the ideal example of the uniform action of his "natural tendency."

Beyond the issue of mathematical representation lies the problem of identifying the force of gravity if it is to replace "natural tendency" and be equated with other forces. In a famous passage Salviati declares that many opinions have been expressed about the cause of acceleration in fall —attraction to the center, the decreasing amount of medium to be penetrated, the closing in of the medium behind the body. "Now, all these fantasies (*fantasie*), and others too, ought to be examined; but it is not really worth while. At present it is the purpose of our Author merely to investigate and to demonstrate some of the properties of accelerated motion (whatever the cause of this acceleration may be). . . ." [26] Galileo's abstention from metaphysical questions to concentrate on the description of motion is much praised by scientists for its positivism, but we should note not only the abstention but also the word he uses to describe suggested explanations. They are "fantasies." He repeats the spirit if not the exact word many times. The notion that the moon and sun influence the tides, he says, "is completely repugnant to my mind; for seeing how this movement of the oceans is a local and sensible one, made by an immense bulk of water, I cannot bring myself to give credence to such causes as lights, warm temperatures,

[26] *Discourses*, pp. 166–167.

predominances of occult qualities, and similar idle imagin-
ings." He refers to such theories again as the "wildest ab-
surdities," and expresses his astonishment that Kepler gave
his assent to the "moon's dominion over the waters, to occult properties, and to such puerilities." [27] Occult qualities
are exactly the problem. Galileo shares, and fully, the seventeenth century's reaction against them. What then about
the downward motion of bodies? If it is not a "natural
tendency," what is it? Descartes and Gassendi are later to
attribute it to the impact of subtle particles. Galileo does
not express himself on the idea, but his conviction that the
acceleration of fall is a constant and that weight is proportional to bulk must rule it out. Perhaps he might ascribe
it to a magnetic action, since Galileo is greatly impressed
by Gilbert's work. Beyond the fact that magnetism would
leave the dilemma unsolved, the objections to such a theory
are so immediate and so obvious that one wonders how anyone could ever have espoused it. Certainly Galileo's discussion of magnetism does not. What else is left except an at-

[27] *Dialogue*, pp. 445, 462. Cf. p. 410. Also *Discourses*, pp. 70–71:
Salviati discusses how water on leaves forms in drops. It cannot be
owing to any internal tenacity acting between the particles. Such a
quality should reveal itself the more when the water is surrounded by
wine in which it is less heavy than it is in air, whereas in fact the drop
collapses when surrounded by wine. The formation of the drop is
owing rather to the pressure of the air with which water has some
incompatibility, which he does not understand. Simplicio breaks in at
this point. Salviati makes him laugh by his efforts to avoid the word
antipathy. Salviati in turn replies ironically, "All right, if it please
Simplicio, let this word antipathy be the solution of our difficulty."
Here Galileo lets it drop, but the passage illustrates beautifully the
contrast between the drive for mechanical explanations on the one
hand (external air pressure, not internal attraction) and the animism he
rejects. His scornful phrase, "this *word* antipathy," underlines his
judgment of the empty quality of the old philosophy of nature, words
divorced from the reality of nature. The mere fact that Galileo puts
the initial jibe into Simplicio's mouth is significant; manifestly Galileo
finds a world of difference between an "antipathy" and "a certain
incompatibility which I do not understand. . . ."

traction?—that is to say, an occult quality? Galileo is
tossed here on the horns of the century's dilemma. Reaction
against the sympathies and antipathies of Renaissance
naturalism renders such a theory impossible, while the drive
for mathematical description makes it necessary. Perhaps
Galileo's abstention from metaphysical discussion is more
embarrassed than deliberate. The advantages of his posture
have been remarked many times. I must insist on the dis-
advantages, which inevitably accompany them. His avoid-
ance of the question of gravity, making impossible its equation with other accelerating actions, is a major obstacle pre-
venting his advance toward a concept of force.

Is the argument above another way of saying that the
phrase "natural tendency" is a mere convention adopted
to avoid the issue of gravity? Galileo's ever repeated sneer
at occult qualities, especially when it is coupled with an
explicit refusal to discuss the cause of gravity, testifies, I
believe, that he is aware of his dilemma. Nevertheless, the
phrase "natural tendency" expresses such a deep and essential current of his thought that it is impossible to imagine
him without it. To adapt the famous undergraduate judgment of Dante and the Renaissance, he stands with one foot
in the old cosmology and with the other greets the dawn
of the new. The very immensity of the step that he takes
places him in a new and alien world, and we must not be
surprised that even a genius of his order finds it necessary
to drag along as many items of intellectual furniture as he
can from the old familiar world. Hence, if we examine his
works carefully for a consistent philosophy of nature, we
are driven to the conclusion that Galileo has bogged down
in a philosophic morass. Its effects appear in his treatment
of motion, in his failure to justify the assertion that a projectile can move at once with a natural tendency and with
an externally impressed motion without the two inhibiting
each other. If there are both natural tendencies and other

motions, can they possibly exist together in the same body wholly indifferent to each other? The question makes no sense to us because we deny the premise. But Galileo does not deny it, and when he consistently refuses to discuss the problem, however much the context demands it, we can only say that he unites the opposites by nothing more than arbitrary assertion. Equally arbitrary is his assertion about the nonoperative and imperceptible quality of motion to those who share it. Could a body fail to be affected by a motion produced by its "natural tendency?" More fundamental yet is the cosmos itself. Halfway committed to the mechanical universe, the impersonal universe of matter in motion, he tries to combine with it the organized cosmos of another philosophy. The fascination that the circle continues to exercise over him is well known. It expresses the still more fundamental conviction that the universe is a "perfect order," "constituted in the best arrangement." [28] Here is the ultimate obstacle in Galileo's thought to a concept of force. The organized cosmos to which he clings refuses to dissolve itself into the mechanical universe from which the concept of force ultimately emerges.

Descartes' judgment of Galileo's mechanics deserves more sympathy than it usually receives—"that without having considered the first causes of nature, he has merely investigated the causes of some particular effects, and thus he has built on sand." [29] Certainly it appears to me that Galileo has taken mechanics to the very limit of its possible advance within his framework. In order to move further, mechanics must now take the bracing plunge into the cold Cartesian bath where the remnants of Aristotelian cosmology can be purged away. It is, after all, Descartes who

[28] *Dialogue*, p. 32.
[29] Descartes to Mersenne, October 11, 1638; *Œuvres de Descartes*, ed. by Charles Adam and Paul Tannery (Paris, 1897–1910), II, 380. 12 vols.

places all motion, as motion, on the same metaphysical plane. Let me not, however, desecrate our commemoration of Galileo with a hymn to the praise of Descartes. If his philosophic rigor in the analysis of motion is a major contribution, like Galileo before him, he, too, sacrifices much to achieve his advance. The cause of gravity is identified with the cause of every other change in motion; all result from the impact of material corpuscles. Where in all this is Galileo's mathematical description of motion? Alas, it is nowhere. Descartes contents himself with verbal descriptions and shows little interest in Galileo's mathematical ones; indeed, it appears impossible to derive them with rigor from Descartes' universe. Thus it remains for Newton at the end of the century to combine genius equal to that of Galileo or of Descartes with the immense good fortune that both of them lived before him. Inheriting both their legacies, he is able to amalgamate them and to complete their work. What does he add to complete it? The concept of force.

V

PUMPS AND PENDULA:
GALILEO AND TECHNOLOGY

Lynn White, Jr.

*B*ECAUSE Galileo is the most influential scientist since Aristotle, much of the controversy over the historical relationship between science and technology naturally has centered around him. Ever since 1927 when the book of my lamented friend, Leonardo Olschki, *Galilei und seine Zeit*,[1] laid the basis for modern studies of Galileo's background and context, much of the learned world has realized that during Galileo's early career—down to his acquisition of the telescope in 1609 at least—his environment and interests were largely technological. There is no profit in repeating in detail how he studied in Florence with the architect and engineer Ostilio Ricci; how he mastered machine design, canal construction, dyking and fortification; how, according to a famous story, he offended Giovanni de' Medici, commander of the fortress and harbor of Livorno, by pointing out the impracticality of a machine the latter had designed; how he owed his professorial appointment in Padua to the recommendation of the great military engineer Guidobaldo del Monte; how in Padua he maintained a personal workshop in his house; and how in 1597 at Venice he patented a water-hoisting engine.

[1] (Halle, 1927), esp. pp. 148–158.

Moreover, since Olschki's work we have not been able to forget that in Galileo's most influential book, the *Discourses* of 1638, Galileo opens the discussion with a dramatic description of the arsenal of Venice as an inspiration to scientific speculation. But is this, perhaps, only a rhetorical device? Galileo was a notable craftsman in literature, and it may be that in fact the Venetian arsenal was as unrelated to the essence of his scientific life as it had been to Dante's poetry and religion when, three centuries earlier, its boiling pitch provided an image in the *Inferno*. Olschki, a man of subtle mind, did not maintain that such technological involvements were the sole, or perhaps even the chief, key to an understanding of the mature Galileo. He insisted merely that the technological element was significant during Galileo's formative period.

After its appearance in 1927, Olschki's work had a curious fortune. Quite against its author's wishes, it provided heavy ammunition for the great Marxist drive of the twenties and thirties to capture the allegiance of intellectuals. Focusing largely on Galileo, Descartes, and Newton, a deluge of books and articles appeared, at vastly varying levels of scholarship and sophistication, by authors ranging alphabetically from Borkenau to Zilsel, all asserting, if not demonstrating, that the science of any historical period is the investigation of theoretical problems raised by contemporary technology, which, in turn, reflects the interests of the ruling group. Seen thus, Galileo becomes a puppet with the Italian bourgeoisie pulling the technological strings.

Doubtless those in this movement who were conscious propagandists hoped that such a thesis would help to put the clerks into psychic blue jeans and give them a sense of unity with the revolutionary proletariat. In any event, the effort largely failed. A high proportion of scientists and historians of science recoiled, with all the quivering primness of a virgin insulted, from the notion that society, through technology, dictates the shape of science.

The counterrevolution of the purists was launched in 1939 with Alexandre Koyré's vastly influential *Études galiléennes*.[2] Although in a parenthesis on his first page Koyré admits the dignity of the history of technology, that is the last we hear of it. In a note to his second page he crushes Francis Bacon's scientific utilitarianism with a vituperation quite uncharacteristic of so gentle a scholar, while in a note to his third page he simply brushes aside the careful erudition of Olschki. Koyré's Galileo is a bit like Jacques Maritain's Aquinas—a vast intellect palpitating in a realm of pure Ideas unsullied by the ὕλη of practical considerations, unaffected by the outer world which pays the bills.[3] Rupert Hall[4] is correct in calling Koyré's position "Platonist, antiempiricist."

It is, of course, a legitimate option to write the history of science in terms of the developing internal tradition of scientific problems and solutions, just as it is proper, if one chooses, to write the history of art that way. Koyré was the supreme master of this approach. Such a method offers unrivaled clarity of definition, and one can therefore understand why Koyré's intellectual manner has become so fashionable as to be orthodox at present among historians of science, especially in America. But absolute clarity may not be the sole virtue in the writing of history. Many prospects are at their best when somewhat clouded. To one like my-

---

[2] (Paris, 1939). 3 vols.

[3] Even eighteen years after his *Études*, Alexandre Koyré's "La dynamique de Niccolò Tartaglia," *La science au seizième siècle: Colloque international de Royaumont, 1957* (Paris, 1960), pp. 93–113, shows him unable to admit technological stimuli to scientific thought: Tartaglia's consideration of dynamics is entirely in terms of cannon and cannonballs, yet to Koyré this is no more than a device of presentation, designed to get the discussion out of its traditional philosophical form.

[4] "Merton Revisited," *History of Science*, II (1963), 16, n. 29.

self, who is not a historian of science, it would seem that although the discipline of the history of science is today winning increasing recognition among philosophers, it is becoming less exciting to general historians, economists, social psychologists, sociologists, and engineers, than it was twenty-five years ago when historians of science were heatedly discussing not only science as a self-contained intellectual activity, but also the nature and extent of science's connections with other human concerns. I fear for the future health of the history of science if it abides in its present faith that all scientific conception is immaculate.

The year 1964 is witnessing a remarkable international smorgasbord of symposia in honor of Galileo; yet, to judge by their anticipatory announcements, what may be called the "Olschki problem" is being massively neglected. The only such colloquium as yet published, far from discussing the possible influence of technology upon Galileo, inverts precedent by including a treatment of "L'influenza di Galileo sullo sviluppo della tecnica." [5] The author of this paper is learned and perceptive, but unfortunately he projects into the seventeenth and eighteenth centuries the twentieth-century relationship between science and technology; moreover, in harmony with the Koyré tradition, he assumes that impulses to progress come entirely from science to technology. Galileo influenced technology, it appears, by elaborating, first, scientific instrumentation, and, second, the mathematical handling of scientific phenomena, both of which were then transferred to technology. The author concludes: "If science and technology had not had the push which came to them from the innovative movement which culminates in Galileo, would there have been a French Revolution?," the implied answer being *no*.

Yet the more probable answer is *yes*. Maurice Daumas, one of the few competent historians of science who have

---

[5] Renato Teani, in *Fortuna di Galileo* (Bari, 1964), pp. 99–125.

also probed the history of technology, has recently insisted on three occasions [6] that the so-called Industrial Revolution of the eighteenth century, which in France made the bourgeoisie at last strong enough to seize power, was an economic or managerial rather than a technological novelty; the technical improvements of the time were merely the contemporary phase of a centuries-long acceleration in technological change. Moreover, as Daumas shows, prior scientific discovery does not play a major part in technological change until the 1850's. Galileo cannot be held responsible for Robespierre.

What then, are we to think of Galileo's relation to technology, both as regards its possible influence upon him and his possible influence upon it? I would suggest that we stand back a bit from the immediate question.

Historically, the connections between science and technology fall into three clusters.[7] First, technology presents problems or experiences that stimulate scientific investigation. Second, scientists develop needs for instruments that technicians then produce; these instruments both aid scientists to new discoveries and give technicians new ideas for further invention. Third, scientific discovery sometimes leads to practical application. Very briefly, let us look at these three aspects of our problem during the later Middle Ages and the Renaissance. Obviously, it is the third that demands our chief attention, since, rightly or wrongly, the

[6] "Rapports entre sciences at techniques: Étude générale du point de vue de l'histoire des sciences et des techniques," *Revue de synthèse*, LXXXIII (1962), 15–37; *Histoire générale des techniques* (Paris, 1962), I, xv; "Le mythe de la révolution technique," *Documents pour l'histoire des techniques*, III (1964), 291–302.

[7] The first two of these are presented as five in Rupert Hall's admirable "The Scholar and the Craftsman in the Scientific Revolution," *Critical Problems in the History of Science*, ed. by Marshall Clagett (Madison, 1959), pp. 3–23.

dependence of the engineer upon the scientist has become an article of faith in our time.

As an enthusiast for medieval technology, I should be pleased if I could offer a considerable list of scientific adventures provoked by medieval craftsmen. But I cannot. The clearest case is the epochal treatise on magnetism written in 1269 by Peter of Maricourt when he was a military engineer in the retinue of Charles of Anjou at the siege of Lucera. The magnetic compass as an aid to navigation had arrived in Europe from China during the 1190's, and without the compass Peter's *Epistola de magnete* is inconceivable. Since Peter's work was completely absorbed into Gilbert's *De magnete* of 1600, 1269 is a great date in the history of science, and one would expect some analogous stimuli from technology to other areas of medieval scientific thought. However, I have not found another entirely convincing instance until the early fifteenth century when, as Giorgio de Santillana has pointed out,[8] Brunelleschi's perspective device and then Alberti's *camera obscura* of about 1430, both produced not as scientific instruments but rather as craftsmen's tools, initiated novel scientific speculations on the nature of light and of vision. Indeed, it is not until the later sixteenth century—the time of Tartaglia, Benedetti, and Stevin—that any considerable number of scientific insights seem to spring from the problems or experiences of engineers.[9]

The truth is that medieval science generally was a very bookish business, conducted by means of abstract thought rather than by experiment. It started with a vast wave of translations from Arabic and Greek in the late eleventh

[8] "The Role of Art in the Scientific Renaissance," *ibid.*, pp. 33–65.

[9] See, most recently, Bertrand Gille, *Les ingénieurs de la Renaissance* (Paris, 1964), pp. 203–222. Contrary to common assumption, the wide application, during the sixteenth century, of mathematics to ballistics and the art of fortification did not lead to basic inventions; it helped to perfect empirical inventions.

century, and its odor remained that of ink and parchment. Indeed, increasing saturation in, and admiration for, ancient writings gave new life to the Greco-Roman view that no scholar would dirty himself with manual operations. The Benedictines, who intellectually dominated the early Middle Ages in the West, were required by their *Rule* both to be educated and to work with their hands. The most perfect written reflection of this attitude is found in the monk Theophilus' treatise on craftsmanship written in 1122–23,[10] just when the tide of translation was rising fast. The revived neoclassical separation of brain from hand emerges clearly in the thirteenth century when the physicians on the faculties of universities withdrew themselves from the surgeons and the apothecaries, both of which groups are inevitably involved in physical activity, however sophisticated.[11]

Medieval science, then, was an autonomous speculative activity, closely connected, through the Muslims and Byzantines, with ancient Greek science and attitudes. Its problems were essentially those inherited from the Greeks. It owed few debts to current technical activity. The miracle is that, despite such encapsulation, by the later thirteenth century, and far more in the fourteenth, these speculative scientists were coming up with radically new modes of thought in mathematics, optics, and physics which provided much of the intellectual framework for Galileo himself. To deny scientific continuity between the fourteenth and the seventeenth centuries is to overlook much of the firmest recent scholarship in the history of science. Yet Buridan is not Galileo, and the chief difference between them would seem to be Galileo's greater sense of

[10] Lynn White, Jr. "Theophilus redivivus," *Technology and Culture*, V (1964), 224–233.

[11] V. L. Bullough, "Status and Medieval Medicine," *Journal of Health and Human Behavior*, II (1961), 204–210.

concrete objects, his instinct for experimental procedures. The seventeenth century shook off the incubus of classical attitudes and once more narrowed the gap between hand and brain. It would be absurd, today, to hold that Galileo's scientific thought was inspired primarily by practical considerations; nevertheless I believe that when Galileo used a description of the Venetian arsenal as the overture to his greatest book, he was deliberately trying to sensitize his readers to the technological sources of the novel element that separated his own scientific methods from those of the past.

The second major connection between technology and science is in scientific instrumentation. As I have said, most medieval science was little interested in experimentation or direct observation; consequently there was no great pressure to develop new instruments. The exception was astronomy, and here the results were spectacular. By at least 1270, astronomers, discontented with water clocks, were demanding a weight-driven mechanical clock. Some sixty years elapsed before the problem was solved with the magnificently ingenious invention of the escapement. Clocks quickly permeated all European life, and the industry that grew up to make and repair these intricate mechanisms provided a broad base for the later development of scientific instrumentation.

Galileo's relation to the increased use of instruments in science—his microscope, his improvement of the geometrical compass, his new hydrostatic balance, his thermoscope, and the like—has been too well explored to need comment here. The dependence of scientist upon craftsman in this area is best symbolized by the fact that his most famous instrument, the telescope, seems to have originated in Holland for nautical and military purposes.

Today, when we speak of science and technology, we think chiefly of their third relationship: the application of scientific discovery to practical ends. From antiquity on, engineers building machines and architects constructing buildings had, of course, used analogue computation to achieve the required sizes.[12] But aside from such operations, the vigorously innovative technology of the Middle Ages shows no trace of the application of consciously scientific principles. It is completely empirical. A medieval student of optics may, indeed, express hope that the sun's rays can be concentrated by new devices so as to burn enemy ships or siege engines, but this is no more than an echo of the stories about Archimedes at the siege of Syracuse. One is tempted to think that since eyeglasses were invented in Tuscany in the 1280's, their inventor may have known about the new lenses that Grosseteste and Roger Bacon had been fondling two or three decades earlier. However, the great excitement that, before 1285, Jean de Meung shows in *Le Roman de la Rose*[13] over both lenses and the curious distorted reflections obtainable in the large lead-backed glass mirrors then becoming available makes one suspect that eyeglasses emerged not by scientific inspiration but from the world of glass-makers and the cutters of glass, gems, and crystal.

How early can one nail down a clear instance of an invention that is the application of a scientific discovery?

I deliberately skirt that Sargasso Sea of the history of navigation, to which theoretical astronomy would seem to have made some contribution by the time of Prince Henry the Navigator. It is my impression, however, that deep into the seventeenth century, especially north of the equator where the polestar offers guidance, most sea captains re-

[12] For an example, cf. G. Beaujouan, "Calcul d'expert, en 1391, sur le chantier du Dôme de Milan," *Le Moyen âge*, LXIX (1963), 555–563.

[13] *Le Roman de la rose*, ed. by E. Langlois (Paris, 1914–1924), lines 16863–16866, 18044–18080, 18152–18286.

mained skilled empiricists using methods almost unaffected by science. When Galileo proposed that his discovery of the moons of Jupiter might aid seamen to determine their longitude, there was a flurry of technical excitement, but nothing practical for mariners ever came of the suggestion.

Galileo was, however, the effective founder of the science of the strength of materials.[14] To be sure, Leonardo had speculated and perhaps even experimented in this area, notably in testing the tensile strength of iron wire, although this aspect of his work seems to have remained hidden from engineers. Galileo's *Discourses,* on the contrary, were so widely read that his results were generally known. Unfortunately I cannot ascertain when his theoretical formulations began to affect the work of practical builders. I suspect that it was much later.

More complex is the history of the harnessing of steam power. From antiquity the pressure of steam had been recognized, and in Galileo's middle years two notable proposals were made to raise water by steam alone: that of Giambattista della Porta in 1606, and that of Salomon de Caus about 1611. The means to a successful steam engine, however, lay in supplementing the expansive force of steam with compression produced by the weight of the air, and in the early phases of the exploration of vacua and atmospheric pressure Galileo was much involved.

The two circumstances in which a man of the early seventeenth century might observe a vacuum were the siphon and the suction pump. The siphon is of Hellenistic origin, but its slant makes measurement of the column of water a bit difficult. A graduate student at the University of California, Los Angeles, has recently shown [15] that in

[14] S. P. Timoshenko, *History of Strength of Materials* (New York, 1953), pp. 11–15.
[15] S. Shapiro, "The Origin of the Suction Pump," *Technology and Culture,* V (1964), 566–574.

Galileo's time the suction pump was relatively new, having been invented in Italy during the second quarter of the fifteenth century. With its vertical barrel, the pump made measurement of the column of water fairly easy.

In a marginal annotation of 1612, Galileo seems to admit the theoretical possibility of a vacuum.[16] However, the first man to understand both vacua and atmospheric pressure was a Dutchman, particularly interested in the operation of the suction pump—Isaac Beeckman, studying at the University of Caen in 1614. Although Beeckman wrote to Mersenne about the vacuum, his views seem to have had no influence. The line of development is found in Italy in the circle of Galileo.

In 1630 the Genoese scholar Giovanni Battista Baliani wrote to Galileo to ask why a siphon over a mound some seventy feet high had failed to work, and Galileo replied that the phenomenon was owing to some attractive force of a vacuum—scarcely a satisfactory explanation, but one still found applied to the suction pump in the *Discourses* of 1638. Galileo himself never understood atmospheric pressure, yet the great experiment of 1643 conducted by his friend and disciple Torricelli, which definitively established the existence of atmospheric pressure, was as much the product of the scientific atmosphere Galileo had established in Italy as of Earth's gaseous ambience.

From Torricelli the sequence to Pascal, von Guericke, Papin, Hooke, and Boyle is clear, culminating, in 1698, in Thomas Savery's construction of a steam and atmospheric engine which was no longer a laboratory model but a working pump. Unfortunately the metallurgical craftsmanship of the times was inadequate to cope with the high pressures that Savery's design needed to raise water from mines, and consequently it was a failure in practice.

---

[16] The materials on vacua and atmospheric pressure are assembled in W. E. Knowles Middleton, *The History of the Barometer* (Baltimore, 1964), pp. 5–32.

The first successful atmospheric steam engine was of course that invented by Thomas Newcomen, a Devonshire ironmonger, who labored at least a decade, from about 1702 to 1712, to produce it. It is inconceivable to our modern minds that such a feat could have been achieved by pure empiricism, and as early as 1797 the myth emerged that papers of the Royal Society proved that Hooke was in touch with Newcomen, told him about Papin's experiments, and advised him on his work. As recently as 1961 an article in *Technology and Culture* presents Newcomen as "a man of learning, versed in science, [who] maintained an active correspondence with Robert Hooke"; and the suggestion is offered that Newcomen "may have actually been employed in the erection of the early Savery engines."[17] Yet patient search, long since, has failed to turn up the slightest evidence to support such assertions. Quite the contrary, a recent and perhaps definitive study of Newcomen[18] shows that contemporaries were as much surprised as we that a provincial craftsman who lacked all contact with, or knowledge of, the Savery engine or the scientific researches on which Savery's work was based, could have solved such a problem as harnessing steam.

Yet Thomas Newcomen clearly was an empirical genius of awesome proportions. His extraordinary invention of the so-called snifting valve, essential to the continuing operation of his engine because it drew off the air that was dissolved in the steam released in the cylinder by the condensation of the steam, could not have been based on science, because scientists in his day were not aware that air dissolves in water. Moreover, the device Newcomen produced for activating his water-injection valves by the motion of the walking beam of his pump is comparable in

[17] M. Kerker, "Science and the Steam Engine," *Technology and Culture*, II (1961), 383–384.

[18] L. T. C. Rolt, *Thomas Newcomen: The Prehistory of the Steam Engine* (London, 1963), pp. 48–57.

ingenuity to the clock escapement, and was a major step in the history of automation. We must conclude, in the present state of the evidence, that the mastery of steam power was a purely technological feat, not influenced by Galilean science.

Finally, what of pendula and the pendulum clock? While the old story that Galileo detected the isochronism of the pendulum by watching the swaying chandelier at Pisa is now abandoned, it is a fact that he discovered it. Historians of science have failed to note that this phenomenon would have been hard to observe earlier than the sixteenth century. As a plaything the swing had been known since antiquity, but it is normally "pumped"; censers in the hands of priests and acolytes seldom oscillate freely for any long time; suspended lamps in the wind move irregularly. Not until the pendulum was applied to machinery could it be closely observed.

From the twelfth century onward, when the flywheel appeared as a method of smoothing out continuous rotary motion in complex machines, the enthusiasm of engineers for converting reciprocating into rotary motion was so dominant that the pendulum, the basic governor for reciprocating motion, was overlooked. Thus far no one has located a pendulum earlier than the late 1490's when Leonardo sketched two of them, one on a reciprocating pump, and another applied to what seems to be an escapement for clockwork. However, it was not until Jacques Besson's *Theatrum instrumentorum et machinarum*, published at Lyons in 1569, with an expanded edition in 1578, that the utility of the pendulum for mechanical saws, bellows, pumps, and polishing machines was clearly envisaged.[19] And it was in the early 1580's that Galileo discovered its isochronism.

[19] There is no adequate history of the pendulum. Some material is assembled in Lynn White, Jr., *Medieval Technology and Social Change* (Oxford, 1962), pp. 117, 172–173.

Yet it was six decades later, in the last months of his life, that the now blind Galileo first thought of applying the pendulum to clockwork, although in 1637 he had constructed a pendulum attached to a train of wheels in order to count its oscillations. In 1641 he talked to his son Vincenzio about a pendulum clock, and Vincenzio has left us a sketch [20] of this remarkable device—prime evidence of the incredible intellectual vitality of the dying titan. It was not until 1649 that Vincenzio tried to build the machine, but he himself died before it was completed. It is listed, still unfinished, among the effects of his wife when she died in 1669. Nevertheless it was not entirely forgotten; in 1656 Prince Leopoldo de' Medici examined this partial model and ordered his court clockmaker Johan Philipp Treffler to complete one. But in 1657 Christian Huygens, working with a skilled clockmaker of The Hague, Solomon Coster, not only made but patented the effective invention of the pendulum clock without inspiration from Galileo.

What, then, is Galileo's relation to technology?

As is shown by his suggestion, repeated to the Netherlands government as late as 1636, that navigation might be aided by observing the moons of Jupiter, Galileo retained throughout his long life at least a marginal concern for the practical application of scientific discoveries. Yet it is astonishing to our twentieth century minds how little impact Galileo and his circle had upon the technology either of their own time or of the following two hundred years. Until the seventeenth century, European technology had been both more sophisticated than European science and little related to that science. The gulf that separates the remarkable metallurgy of Biringuccio, Agricola, and Ercker from the neoalchemy of contemporary theorizing about metals, illustrates the general situation. During the

[20] F. J. Britten, *Old Clocks and Watches and Their Makers*, 7th ed. (London, 1956), p. 67, plate 41.

seventeenth century pure science made vast strides, led, in physics and astronomy, by Galileo. Moreover, even in the sixteenth century we find an increasing number of men who, like Galileo, combined scientific with technical interests. But the millennial separation of scientist from engineer, of thinker from craftsman, could not be ended in a generation. It remained dominant for another two centuries and is not vanished even in our own time.

In the field of scientific instrumentation—and the pendulum clock, for example, was conceived primarily as an aid to science—it is clear to the point of platitude that Galileo was not only an inventor but the greatest of propagandists for the use of hardware in scientific investigation.

Finally, we must conclude that while the fruits of Galileo's thought were harvested by pure science rather than by technology, Olschki was correct in saying that his intellectual roots lay not only in the alluvium of inherited speculative and mathematical science but also in the contemporary engineering. Yet the development of the history of technology enables us to see a little further today than could Olschki in 1927. He could scarcely have learned, for example, that the suction pump was so recent in Galileo's time, or that the first major presentation of the pendulum in machine design had been published only a dozen years before Galileo observed its isochronism. Art has always been a highly selective mirror of nature. We can now see that the rapidly expanding mechanic arts of Galileo's age —in his own metaphor, the Venetian arsenal—provided novel controlled situations, almost laboratory situations, in which he could be among the first to observe natural phenomena, like isochronism or the breaking of a column of water, which are not easily perceived in a pure state of nature. It is exactly Galileo's environment of technical innovations like suction pumps and pendula which makes the tonality of his new sciences historically intelligible.